To my students in psychology,
past, present, and future

Their influence is
perpetually stimulating
frequently challenging
painfully humbling
and deeply appreciated.

GRATION OF

OLOGY

by Gary R. Collins

CHRISTIANITY

Tyndale House Publishers, Inc. Wheaton, Illinois

LIBRARY OF CONGRESS CATALOG CARD NUMBER 76-47299
ISBN 0-8423-5314-3, CLOTH; 0-8423-5315-1, PAPER
COPYRIGHT © 1977 BY TYNDALE HOUSE PUBLISHERS, INC.,
WHEATON, ILLINOIS 60187. ALL RIGHTS RESERVED.
THIRD PRINTING, MAY 1980.
PRINTED IN THE UNITED STATES OF AMERICA.

DISCARD

The Rebuilding of
PSYCHOLOGY

AN INTE

The
Rebuilding
of
PSYCH

PSYCHOLOGY AND

Acknowledgments

I am very grateful for the time, effort, and helpful comments of a number of people who read portions of this book prior to its publication and made suggestions for its improvement. Each of these suggestions was carefully considered and many were adopted as the manuscript was repeatedly revised. I especially appreciate the critical comments of David Wells, Clark Pinnock, William Sisterson, Bruce Narramore, and my wife Julie. Dean Kenneth S. Kantzer and the administration of Trinity Evangelical Divinity School made it possible for me to spend several months at Cambridge University where the initial draft of this book was prepared, and subsequently, portions of the manuscript were discussed in lively seminars with students and professional colleagues at Philhaven Hospital in Pennsylvania, Rosemead Graduate School of Psychology in California, Georgia State University in Atlanta, University of Wisconsin in Milwaukee, and Trinity Evangelical Divinity School in Illinois. In addition, I want to thank Vivian Ahlberg, Ruth Rodquist, Judy Whiting, and Georgette Sattler who typed and retyped the manuscript, and my graduate assistant, Larry Tornquist, who worked on proofreading and compiling the index.

Finally, acknowledgment is made to the following publishers who gave permission for the reprinting of excerpts from previously published works:

American Psychological Association—for excerpts from Nevitt Sanford, "Will Psychologists Study Human Problems?" *American Psychologist*, 20, 1965.

Comprehensive Psychiatry—for excerpts from Orville S. Walters, "Religion and Psychopathology," 101, 1964.

Concordia Publishing House—for excerpts from P. Meehl, *et al.,* *What, Then, Is Man?* 1958.

William B. Eerdmans Publishing Co.—for excerpts from E. J. Carnell, *An Introduction to Christian Apologetics,* 1948; and G. C. Berkouwer, *Man: The Image of God,* 1962.

Harper & Row Publishers, Inc.—for excerpts from A. H. Maslow, *Toward a Psychology of Being,* 1962; A. H. Maslow, *Motivation and Personality* (second edition), 1970; and Paul Tournier, *The Person Reborn,* 1966.

Inter-Varsity Press—for excerpts from J. W. Montgomery, *The Altizer-Montgomery Dialogue,* 1967; and Malcolm Jeeves, *The Scientific Enterprise and Christian Faith,* 1969.

Jonathan Cape, Ltd—for excerpts from Liam Hudson, *The Cult of the Fact,* 1972 (published in the U.S. by Harper Torchbooks, 1973).

The Macmillan Co.—for excerpts from Gordon Allport, *The Individual and His Religion,* 1950.

McGraw-Hill Book Co., Inc.—for excerpts from James F. T. Bugental (ed.), *Challenges of Humanistic Psychology,* 1967.

Moody Press—for excerpts from Clark H. Pinnock, *Set Forth Your Case,* 1967.

Penguin Books, Inc.—for excerpts from Robert Thompson, *The Pelican History of Psychology,* 1968.

Prentice-Hall, Inc.,—for excerpts from Duane P. Schultz (ed.), *The Science of Psychology: Critical Reflections,* 1970.

Psychology Today—for excerpts from David Bakan, "Psychology can now kick the science habit," March 1972.

Random House, Inc.—for excerpts from Joseph Wood Krutch, *Human Nature and the Human Condition,* 1959.

John Wiley & Sons, Inc.—for excerpts from Allen E. Bergin and Sol L. Garfield (ed.), *Handbook of Psychotherapy and Behavior Change,* 1971.

Word Incorporated—for excerpts from R. Bube, *The Human Quest,* 1971.

University of Chicago Press—for excerpts from T. W. Wann (ed.), *Behaviorism and Phenomenology,* 1964.

Contents

Chapter One

PSYCHOLOGY

IN A
DILEMMA

3   PSYCHOLOGY today is alive and flourishing. The evidence is all around. Books on psychology, both technical and popular, are rolling off the presses and are eagerly bought by professionals and lay people alike. Psychology courses are popular parts of the college curriculum. Enrollment of graduate students in psychology is increasing at a rate that impressively outdistances every other scientific discipline.[1] In North America there is hardly a medical school, theological seminary, or teachers' college that does not require students to have at least some exposure to the "science of human behavior." The research findings of psychology and the pronouncements of psychologists have affected business, advertising, social work, nursing, and engineering. Psychologists are influential in mental hospitals, industries, schools, and military establishments. Politicians use psychological techniques for "selling themselves" to voters. Prison officials look to psychologists for assistance in rehabilitating offenders. Most of the social issues of our age—ecology, poverty, racism, international diplomacy, aging, education, violence, crime, drug abuse, pornography, war, disease—are studied by psychologists who work with professionals of other disciplines in an attempt to find solutions for human problems.

This is remarkable progress when one realizes that scientific psychology is only 100 years old. It was during the 1870s that Wilhelm Wundt set out to make psychology an independent and self-sufficient academic discipline. In one room at the University of Leipzig in Germany, Wundt established what is generally considered to be the first psychological laboratory. Most of the early leaders in psychology took their training there, although it was not until the end of the century that the young science began to make its influence felt throughout the universities of western Europe and America.

When the first convention of the American Psychological Association (APA) was held early in the 1890s, fewer than twenty people were present. Today APA has almost 40,000 members, roughly one-third of whom

4

gather each year for the annual meeting of their profession. The elementary and somewhat crude experimental techniques of Wundt's time have given way to sophisticated research designs, rooms full of elaborate apparatus, and computerized analyses of data. Outside the profession many people look upon psychology with a sense of awe. Many would probably agree with an enthusiastic reporter for *Life* magazine who several years ago wrote that we now live in an Age of Psychology which has had a "spectacular" beginning and is certain to experience great expansion in the future.

Such enthusiasm is not limited to the general public or to professional journalists. In his presidential address to the APA, Kenneth B. Clark argued that the critical sciences today are the behavioral sciences. He asserted that "a rigorous, tough-minded" psychology is what the world needs in order to save mankind and insure survival of the human race. Religion, moral philosophy, law, and education are powerless to control man's primitive and egocentric behavior. In place of these ineffective solutions, social sciences like psychology must help people to control their "animalistic, barbaric, and primitive" tendencies so that the "uniquely human ... characteristics of love, kindness, and empathy" can shine forth.[2] An earlier APA president was even more enthusiastic. He described scientific psychology as "potentially one of the most revolutionary intellectual enterprises ever conceived by the mind of man,"[3] and he went on to propose that we need to "give psychology away" so that its techniques for promoting human welfare can be available to anyone who wants to use them.

A lot of people, however, are beginning to wonder if psychologists have very much to give away. Students and some of their professors are coming to realize that psychology may not have so much to offer as its more enthusiastic supporters claim. We talk of our "tough-minded science" and predict that it will save the world, but have we shown that psychology is that powerful? We proclaim the rigor and relevance of our

5 discipline, but isn't it possible that much of what we give to others is "metapsychology"—extrascientific preconceptions and untested personal opinions of dubious scientific validity?[4] We delight in psychology's wide popularity, but after a century of research has there been significant progress toward a better understanding of behavior? Even with our best efforts it seems that we have uncovered few laws of behavior; and our methods, admirable as they may be, still leave much to be desired. Instead of developing into a coherent and unified science, psychology has become overly specialized and split into a vast collection of conflicting techniques, problems, theories, and unrelated bits of data. It is hardly surprising, therefore, that some psychologists and students have begun to wonder if they are involved in a crumbling discipline, a science that appears on the surface to be in the best of health, but is actually in imminent danger of collapse.[5]

Over the years there have been many criticisms of psychology, but four weaknesses have been mentioned repeatedly. The first of these is that psychology has a bad public image. Undoubtedly there are people who still think that psychology is "just common sense," that it is preoccupied with sex, and that psychologists are all unstable people who don't know how to solve their personal problems or control their unruly children. Although there may be an element of truth in these criticisms, they are largely unfounded prejudices which fortunately are disappearing from the minds of the general public. More serious are charges that psychological devices such as personality tests and research questionnaires invade privacy and restrict individual freedom. Others fear that psychologists are inventing powerful and effective tools for controlling human behavior—tools that could easily be used by unethical businessmen, political candidates, or government officials to manipulate unsuspecting or uncooperative citizens. Most psychologists could give a convincing defense against these charges, but our critics are not easily

6

persuaded, especially if they are inclined to distrust whatever psychologists say.[6]

A second frequent criticism is that psychology is irrelevant. Students, of course, have been saying this for years. They enroll in a general psychology course expecting to learn why people act as they do, but the course often turns out to be a boring recitation of minute and seemingly endless facts largely dealing with the actions of pigeons, white rats, and unenthusiastic college sophomores.[7] Psychology majors and graduate students frequently share this frustration over the seeming irrelevance of their discipline—as do some of psychology's most respected leaders. "If we do not assess the relevance of our work," a well-known psychologist recently wrote, "others certainly will.... Why should we psychologists, who cannot resolve conflicts on our own campuses or run our own professional associations more satisfactorily than any other discipline, suddenly claim that our work will solve the far more difficult problems of urban decay, racial conflict, foreign relations, public education, or mental health?"[8] In order to be intrinsically worthwhile, of course, a science need not always be practical and applicable to human needs, but psychology is a science of behavior, especially human behavior, and one of its oft-stated goals is the promotion of human welfare. To be sure, we have made advances in the direction of this goal. But psychology's critics may be right in their assertion that progress has been remarkably slow and that our science hasn't become very relevant even after a century of research.

A third problem in psychology concerns methodology. From the time of Wundt and perhaps even before, psychologists have been concerned about establishing their discipline as a bona fide science. Many college teachers still fight to convince their students and faculty colleagues in other disciplines that psychology is scientific. Long ago it was decided that if we are to be viewed as scientists we must act like scientists and use generally accepted scientific techniques. Perhaps more than any other discipline, therefore, psychology has taken great pains to develop an effective methodology. To insure that they would be scientific, psychological research procedures were modeled largely on the techniques of established sciences such as physics, chemistry, and physiology. Techniques of natural science have not always worked well in the study of human behavior, but many psychologists have been reluctant to modify or give up methods that are so widely respected and have been developed so laboriously. This methodological rigidity has opened us to the charge that psychologists are more concerned about proper technique than about studying meaningful and relevant psychological issues. Perhaps nobody has stated this problem more clearly than Nevitt Sanford. ''Psychology is really in the doldrums right now,'' he wrote,

> it is fragmented, overspecialized, method centered, and dull. I can rarely find in the journals anything that I am tempted to read. And when I do read psychological papers, as I must as an editorial consultant, I become very unhappy; I am annoyed by the fact that they all have been forced into the same mold, in research design and style of reporting, and I am appalled by the degree to which an inflation of jargon and professional baggage has been substituted for psychological insight and sensitivity....
>
> We have produced a whole generation of research psychologists who never had occasion to look closely at any one person, let alone themselves, who have never imagined what it might be like to be a subject in one of their experiments, who, indeed, have long since lost sight of the fact that their experimental subjects are, after all, people. (Let us leave the rats out of it for a moment.) They can define variables, state hypotheses, design experiments, manipulate data statistically, get publishable results—and miss the whole point of the

8

thing. Reading their papers you get a strange sense of the unreality of it all; the authors' conceptions of variables and processes seem a bit off; and then you realize that the authors have never looked at human experience, they went straight from the textbook or journal to the laboratory, and thence into print—and thence into the business of getting research grants.

The plain fact is that our young psychological researchers do not know what goes on in human beings and their work shows it.... Scientists write for each other; and when they are looking for a problem to investigate, they turn to their professional journals rather than ask such questions as what might be troubling college presidents.[9]

Growing out of this problem of methodology is the fourth criticism—that psychology is too fragmented and overly specialized. Students in big universities are especially inclined to complain about this when they see psychology professors interested in their own narrow sphere of research but with little appreciation for, much less understanding of or interest in, the activities of their colleagues. This problem, which extends far beyond the university community, was highlighted when another APA president, George Albee, proposed that the discipline of psychology has no alternative but to divide formally into at least two camps: scientific psychology and professional psychology. Albee noted that already conflicts and "basic incompatibilities" exist among the various branches of psychology, and he expressed fear that there could be even greater "stress, hostility, charges, and countercharges" in the future unless something is done to deal with this problem.[10]

Modern psychology, therefore, is in a state of flux and faced with a dilemma about its future. The profession is growing in size but losing support from the agencies that grant funds for research and training. In spite of frequent

9

calls for greater relevance, the field seems to be concentrating more and more on minor issues that are of limited practical value.

So, where do we go from here? Does psychology have a bright future, or is it going to have to fight for survival? Can it speak to the problems of our age, or must it be passed off as largely irrelevant? Can psychology contribute significantly to the understanding and betterment of society, or is it destined to live in an ivory tower or on the back wards of the psychiatric hospital?

These questions have important implications for many people. First, there are psychologists themselves, especially the younger ones, who are concerned about their careers and the health of their profession. Then there are students who are beginning careers and planning for the future. Nobody wants to be involved in a splintered or irrelevant discipline, especially in our time. Psychology students need to know if the science of human behavior is going to slip into the doldrums or forge ahead as a powerful force in the future. The question of psychology's direction is also important to the society in which we live. The problems of today—racism, war, crime, violence, industrial and student dissatisfaction, drug abuse, the economy, poverty, the cities, even pollution—are basically human problems. These have been caused by people and they must be solved by people. Fortunately the solutions are not left in the hands of any one discipline. All branches of science, government, humanities, and religion must work on the problems together. But if psychologists who claim to be specialists in human behavior are unable to shed significant light on human dilemmas, then the future of their science and perhaps of the whole society is indeed dark and uncertain.

The future direction of psychology is a topic to which more and more psychologists are directing their attention. This concern is in itself a promising sign that the discipline is alive and moving. Psychologists have noted

10   that the problems of their profession are not unique. Most, perhaps all, of the sciences are facing reductions in research funds, public skepticism over the value of science, awareness that research efforts might be unimportant or irrelevant, and concern that their disciplines are becoming too specialized and method-centered. Like their colleagues in other fields, many psychologists have tried to face these and other weaknesses and do something about them. Convention speeches,[11] seminars, journal articles, and books have tried to clarify the problems and suggest ways to resolve them.

Proposed solutions generally fall into four categories. First, some have suggested, mostly in jest, that we should scrap psychology altogether. It has outlived whatever usefulness it had, one psychologist remarked in a humorous but thought-provoking speech, so perhaps we need to divide it up among the biologists, sociologists, psychiatrists, theologians, philosophers, and others who feel that we are already bungling into their domains.[12] The suggestion that we disband psychology is not likely to be taken seriously, especially by the thousands of psychologists who would be subsequently unemployed. But the idea at least sets us thinking.

A second solution is not much better, but seems to be the route that a large minority are taking: we should maintain the status quo and carry on as we have in the past. Such an idea doesn't get into print very often, because the psychologists who believe this rarely think about the problems within their profession and almost never write about them. Occasionally there is an angry rebuttal that the critics of psychology should spend less time criticizing and more time doing research, but usually the defenders of the status quo plug on, oblivious to the voices of dissent and criticism being raised around them.

A third solution, embraced by perhaps a majority in the field, is that we should stick with existing psychology but try to sharpen its methodology and clarify its

11

direction. How we do this is a matter for debate, but many people are working on the problem. Such a solution, because of its popularity, deserves a careful analysis, which we plan to give in chapters 2 and 3. First we will look at experimental psychology, considering some of its past accomplishments, discussing its weaknesses, and attempting to evaluate its prospects for the future. Then we will turn our attention to clinical and applied psychology. In each of these areas we must ask if a sharpened methodology, a clearer direction, and an increased body of data can provide the best hope for psychology's future.

A <u>fourth</u> solution is more startling in that it calls for a radical change in the aims, methods, and direction of psychology. This alternative, most clearly expressed by members of a growing movement known as "third force" or humanistic psychology, will be discussed in chapter 4.

At this point in our discussion one thing should be evident. In the following pages I don't plan to write a requiem for psychology. I believe that psychology is far from dead. It is true that the discipline has problems and is facing a dilemma about the direction it should take in the future. But solving problems and untangling dilemmas is our business. I am optimistic enough to believe that psychology has the potential for a bright, lively, and productive future. The chapters that follow are written in an attempt to help us move in that direction.

Footnotes
Chapter 1

[1]In a National Scientific Foundation survey of 2,579 academic doctoral departments, the only areas of science showing an increase (between 1970 and 1971) in first year graduate student enrollments were social science (up .04%) and psychology (4.20%). The percent increase in first year doctoral level psychology students has subsequently been even greater. See report in *APA Monitor* **3,** August 1972 and Albee, George W., "The Uncertain Future of Psychology," *APA Monitor* **4,** June 1973, pp. 3, 10. In a more recent report *(APA Monitor* **6,** August 1975) it was noted that "while enrollments declined in the 13 other scientific and technical

12

disciplines, full-time psychology enrollments increased 25 percent from 1968-1973."

[2]Clark, Kenneth B. "The Pathos of Power: A Psychological Perspective," *American Psychologist* **26**, 1971, pp. 1047-1057.

[3]Miller, George A. "Psychology as a Means of Promoting Human Welfare," *American Psychologist* **24**, 1969, pp. 1063-1075.

[4]Smith, M. Brewster. "Is Psychology Relevant to New Priorities?" *American Psychologist* **28**, 1973, pp. 463-471.

[5]The concern that psychologists feel about their own discipline is reflected in the titles of some recent articles in the *American Psychologist*. See, for example, Albee, George W., "The Uncertain Future of Clinical Psychology," **25**, 1970, pp. 1071-1080; Lockard, R. B., "Reflections on the Fall of Comparative Psychology," **26**, pp. 168-179; Silverman, Irwin, "Crisis in Social Psychology: The Relevance of Relevance," **26**, 1971, pp. 583-4; and Baron, Jonathan, "Is Experimental Psychology Relevant?" **26**, 1971, pp. 713-716.

[6]Some of these public criticisms of psychology are discussed in Miller, George A., "Assessment of Psychotechnology," *American Psychologist,* **25**, 1970, pp. 991-1001.

[7]The preoccupation of psychologists with white rats is convincingly demonstrated in articles by Beech, Frank A., "The Snark Was a Boojum," *American Psychologist* **5**, 1950, pp. 115-124; and Bitterman, M. E., "Toward a Comparative Psychology of Learning," *American Psychologist* **15**, 1960, pp. 704-712.

[8]The quotation is from Miller, 1970, *op. cit.,* p. 995. Articles calling for greater relevance in psychology include those by Silverman, *op. cit.,* Baron, *op. cit.,* Smith, *op. cit.,* and a paper by Walker, Edward L., "Relevant Psychology Is a Snark," *American Psychologist* **25**, 1970, pp. 1881-1886.

[9]Sanford, Nevitt. "Will Psychologists Study Human Problems?" *American Psychologist* **20**, 1965, pp. 192, 194. See also Maslow, A. H., "Problem-Centering vs. Means-Centering in Science," *Philosophy of Science* **13**, 1946, pp. 326-331.

[10]See Albee, *op. cit.,* 1970, pp. 1078, 1080. Dr. Albee's conclusions are challenged in Schneider, Stanley, F., "Reply to Albee's 'The Uncertain Future of Clinical Psychology,' " *American Psychologist* **26**, 1971, pp. 1058-1070. See also Wildman, R. W. and Wildman, R. W., II. "The Uncertain Present and Future of Clinical Psychology: A Review and Comments." *The Clinical Psychologist* **27**, Summer, 1974, pp. 19-22.

[11]An example is Leona Tyler's presidential address to the APA. See Tyler, L.E., "Design for a Hopeful Psychology," *American Psychologist* **28**, 1973, pp. 1021-9.

[12]MacLeod, R. B. "The Teaching of Psychology and the Psychology We Teach," *American Psychologist* **20**, 1965, pp. 344-352.

Chapter Two

PSYCHOLOGY

IN THE LABORATORY

WHEN Professor Wundt established his new psychological laboratory, he was faced with the problem of deciding what the new discipline should be like. What does one study in a psychological laboratory? What methods does one use? What are the experiments supposed to show?

Like other scholars of his day, Wundt reached the conclusion that psychology should be concerned with conscious awareness. He wanted to know how people experience such things as sounds, colors, optical illusions, feelings, or words. To find out, the early psychologists made use of a technique known as *introspection*. Subjects were brought into the laboratory and presented with stimulations that were given one at a time. A series of tones might be sounded, for example, which differed from one another in loudness or pitch, and as the subject listened he tried to "observe the state of his consciousness" (this subjective observation was what the early researchers meant by introspection) before giving a verbal description of what he had experienced. The subject would tell which of several sounds was loudest or highest in pitch and then he would listen while the tones were presented several times again so that the experimenter could check the consistency of the subject's observations. Wundt did hundreds of experiments of this type and with his students he analyzed the data and looked for laws to account for the "mental processes" he was trying to observe.

This new introspectionist psychology had its conception and birth in Europe, but its greatest growth occurred in the United States. Since most of the early American psychologists trained in Leipzig, the introspective techniques and findings were carried back across the Atlantic. E. B. Titchener, the influential and articulate experimental psychologist at Cornell, propagated the Wundtian approach with enthusiasm and for more than two decades set a rigorous standard of excellence against which other psychologists matched their work.[1] Before long, however, even the most

16   dedicated students of Wundt and Titchener began to
realize that German introspectionism was too narrow,
subjective, and unproductive. Knowledge did not seem to
be accumulating very quickly—especially when one
compared psychology with more established sciences
like physics or physiology—and the results of
psychological experiments often could not be replicated.
Darwin had already demonstrated that one could study
individual animals (of which man was one) by methods
that did not make use of introspection at all. A
controversial Austrian psychiatrist named Sigmund Freud
(whose first public lectures on the theory of
psychoanalysis had been given in the United States) was
claiming that it was not even possible for an individual
accurately to observe his own mental life. It was hardly
surprising, therefore, that various "schools" or
movements rose up within psychology to protest against
the experimental techniques of Wundt, Titchener, and
their followers. One of these schools, Functionalism,
helped to shift the emphasis in psychology away from
studies of inner consciousness and toward the
investigation of overt actions. But it was the *behaviorism*
of John B. Watson that decisively sounded the death knell
for introspectionism and gave psychology a "fresh clean
start" as a "purely objective experimental branch of
natural science."[2]

Behaviorism was put forth as a deliberate attempt to
sweep aside the method of introspection with its
concern for conscious awareness, and to make
psychology a study of overt, observable behavior. Terms
like "mind," "temperament," "will," or "consciousness"
were cast aside as being of no interest to psychology
since they referred to things that could be inferred but
never observed scientifically. The followers of Watson
preferred to focus their attention on what could be seen
clearly by independent viewers.

Most of the early behavioristic work concentrated on
finding how individuals would react or respond
behaviorally when presented with a stimulus. This was

17 known as stimulus-response or S-R psychology. Nobody asked the subject to tell introspectively how he felt when, for example, a noise was sounded. The experimenters simply watched the subject to see how he responded or how his body reacted physiologically. There was great interest in conditioning studies similar to those done by Pavlov, and the behaviorists devoted long hours to the investigation of how people and animals learn.

In spite of some strong initial opposition, behaviorism came to be accepted by most psychologists, especially in the United States. It was clearly scientific, it permitted psychology to be objective, and it created hope that the science of behavior could forge ahead to a brighter future.

But progress was disappointingly slow in the years that followed. By the late 1920s, fifteen years after Watson had first proposed his behaviorism, psychology was still without any generally accepted principles of behavior. There was a lot of experimentation, but to many people it seemed aimless and not very significant.[3] Once again some envious psychological eyes were cast in the direction of natural science, especially physics, where it was discovered that a philosophy known as *logical positivism* had taken hold.

Briefly stated, logical positivism was the view that the only knowledge worth anything is knowledge that "rests on public experimental verification rather than on personal experience."[4] The experimental method was considered to be the only legitimate procedure, and ideas that could not be tested by public observation were rejected as meaningless and of no value. Positivists had no interest in things like subjective reports about how people feel, theories about the universe, or beliefs about God. Instead, positivism was an attempt to focus attention on observable data and thus to avoid the disagreements that had arisen whenever scientists had tried to make sense of subjective introspective reports. All of this, of course, was consistent with what the behaviorists had been thinking for several years, and it is not surprising that positivism became the "philosophy of science" that was embraced by American psychologists.

One of the outgrowths of the logical positivist philosophy was the development of a new technique. *Operationalism* (or *operationism*) was first proposed by a physicist named Percy Bridgman, who argued that scientists should not waste time making up complicated and subjective verbal definitions of what they were trying to study. Instead, he suggested, the only way for science to investigate things objectively was by defining all of its ideas and concepts with reference to the operations or methods used to measure the concept. Length, for example, could be "defined" by how something is measured with a yardstick or ruler.

The doctrine of operationism quickly caught the imagination of psychologists. S. S. Stevens, who was both a positivist and a colleague of Bridgman's at Harvard, optimistically predicted that operationism would insure against "hazy, ambiguous, and contradictory notions" in psychology and would cure the "notable instability" in the field.[5] "Let us not waste time trying to agree on verbal definitions of, say, intelligence," the operationalists argued. "We will agree instead that intelligence is simply what some intelligence test measures. Maybe we can't arrive at a formal definition which everyone accepts but we all are able to observe and concur on how a test is given and for purposes of discussion we can agree that intelligence is that which is measured by the intelligence test." In the same way, learning came to be defined operationally by reference to the number of trials that a rat took to run a maze without making any errors, or the speed with which a college student could memorize a list of words.

Students today still shake their heads in amazed disbelief when they first learn about operational definitions. To many it must sound like Humpty Dumpty talking to Alice in Wonderland:

"When I use a word," Humpty Dumpty said in

19

rather a scornful tone, "it means just what I choose it to mean—nothing more nor less."

"The question is," said Alice, "whether you can make words mean so many different things."

Although there were weaknesses with the concept of operationism,[6] this technique nevertheless enabled psychology to get on with the business of observation and measurement. Soon there was a growing interest in statistics, and psychologists attempted more and more to express research findings in numbers. Later a learning theorist named Clark Hull wrote a paper in which he proposed a procedure known as the *hypothetico-deductive method*. He maintained that we should begin every piece of research by formulating explicit hypotheses which are then tested experimentally. If the tests don't show what was predicted, then the hypotheses must be revised and retested; if the tests support the hypotheses, these can be added, at least temporarily, to the body of scientific knowledge. Such a procedure has guided research in psychology departments for over forty years.

Since the time of the second world war, behaviorism and experimental psychology in general have been considerably modified. There has, for example, been a return to the old problems of inner feeling, thinking, or sensation; S-R psychology has been largely replaced by an interest in the physiology of the organism which receives the stimulus and does the responding; more sophisticated apparatus and techniques of analyses have been developed; and there is a new interest in making experimental psychology more relevant and concerned with the practical problems of our troubled society.[7]

Yet in spite of this apparent progress people persist in asking the disturbing question of whether anything significant has been or is being accomplished in experimental psychology. The avalanche of research

20   funds available only a few years ago has been reduced to a trickle, and scientists—including psychologists—who want to continue doing research are being forced to examine themselves and to justify their relevance.

Has experimental psychology shown that it has made such worthwhile progress that it ought to continue? After presenting a detailed history of psychology, a British writer recently concluded that in

> looking back one might be tempted to be pessimistic over the development of psychology. The results of research are often tentative or open to question. There have been false starts; grand-scale systems have flourished which are now extinct; precise but futile experiments have often appeared in the journals and monographs; there has been muddled thinking which has drifted off into metaphysics or amateur sociology. Yet there has also been slow but definite progress.[8]

Thanks largely to the theory of behaviorism, psychology has developed a number of objective and reliable experimental methods. Much has been learned about the behavior of animals, and some solid conclusions have been reached at least about such narrow aspects of human behavior as learning or perception. Psychological research has clarified and solved practical "human engineering" problems in industry and the military, and we have discovered some valuable principles of group dynamics.

As noted in the preceding chapter, however, experimental psychology is being criticized even by some of its most devoted followers. There are those who would challenge the conclusion that we are making "definite progress" or that we have done so in the past. Psychological researchers in laboratories and universities have been criticized for being so busy with their research—often with pigeons, rats, college students, and other unwilling, poorly chosen

21   representatives of humanity—that they fail to realize that much of what they are doing may be irrelevant, insignificant, and a foolish waste of time, money, energy, and brain power.

Several years ago a group of distinguished psychologists came together for a conference in which they discussed the present and future direction of scientific psychology. Much of the debate concerned the contemporary value of behaviorism. Although the first speaker attacked it as a "position that was never *seriously* tenable, never consistent, based on thin and shifting rationales,...adapted more to serve needs for comfort and security than a passion for knowledge,...unfruitful,... ludicrous,...(and) defunct,"[9] others clearly disagreed. In several sessions of heated discussion the participants showed, if nothing else, that behaviorism is still a thriving and powerful force in psychology.[10]

Consider, for example, the conclusions of B. F. Skinner. He has been acclaimed by his friends as the most important psychologist of the century, and even his many critics acknowledge that his work has been of great influence and importance. Skinner's creative experiments with animals demonstrated the value of what he termed "reinforcement." His findings led him to invent the teaching machine and to put forth some controversial ideas about education. He wrote a best-selling novel, *Walden Two,* in which he demonstrated how whole cultures could be redesigned if the principles of reinforcement were consistently applied. Skinner's work ranks him as one of the most productive and creative psychologists of all time, but his books and articles show that he is also one of the firmest believers in behaviorism. "I am a radical behaviorist," Skinner has said, "in the sense that I find no place...for anything which is mental."[11] He claims to have no interest in theorizing about behavior or in trying to explain why people act as they do. Instead, Skinner believes in observing behavior and describing how observable stimuli bring about observable responses. This, he

22   believes, is the only way that psychology can be
scientific and it is the only hope for its advancement.

Behaviorism is vulnerable to criticism, however, and
so therefore is much of contemporary experimental
psychology. The protests tend to come from four
sources: humanism, philosophy, physics, and psychology
itself.

The *humanistic protest* complains that behaviorism
ignores and often denies man's uniquely human
characteristics. For the strict behaviorist, man is something
like a machine: an organism with actions that are
completely lawful, predictable, and controlled by
environmental influences. Since man is manipulable
and influenced primarily by external stimulation it would
seem to follow that he has no real individual autonomy,
no responsibility, and no ability to control his future. He
is, according to Skinner, a being that has neither
freedom nor dignity.[12]

This conclusion puts the psychological researcher into
an awkward and uncomfortable position. Since he
assumes that all human behavior is completely
controlled by environmental forces, he must conclude that
the human subjects in his experiments really have no
freedom to act independently; but neither does the
human experimenter. He cannot stand apart from the
human race. He too must be completely controlled and
lacking in freedom. It is hardly surprising that the
behavioristic view has been strongly attacked and
severely criticized as a theory "difficult to apply to
others...but impossible to apply to oneself."[13]

Those who believe in man's freedom and capacity for
self-determination maintain that human beings are more
than complex reacting machines or impersonal objects
that can be psychologically dissected and analyzed by
behavioristic techniques. On the contrary, man is seen
as a creature of value and dignity; a person who, though
influenced by his environment, is nevertheless able to
plan his own actions, to shape his own future, and to look

23

after his own welfare—all in ways that experimental psychology can neither measure nor predict.

In response to such criticisms the behaviorist protests that he like everyone else is concerned about human welfare and that his efforts are an attempt to show how people can more efficiently improve themselves.[14] Skinner, for example, insists that although human beings are completely controlled by environmental influences and thus are lacking in freedom, they somehow are at the same time free to mold the environment that will control them and to apply the principles of reinforcement in a way that will bring about a utopian society.[15] This conclusion, of course, rests on the dubious assumption that the techniques of reinforcement will be used for the betterment of all mankind and not merely for the personal advantage of the controllers.

Closely related to the humanistic protests are some *philosophical criticisms* of behaviorism. As we have seen, the strict behaviorist accepts the philosophical assumption that every part of man's psychological nature expresses itself in behavior that can be objectively observed by others. If things like feelings, desires, attitudes, motives, thoughts, expectations, moral values, and other "mental states" actually exist, the behaviorist asserts, they will reveal themselves in observable behavior. Because of this we should get on with the job of studying behavior and quit wasting time trying to uncover "indwelling agents that probably do not exist and wouldn't explain anything if they did." Skinner complains that mankind has spent 2,500 years in a futile search for some internal mental causes of our actions and he, for one, would prefer now to put aside the whole idea of mental states and turn to what in his opinion is a more productive approach: the study of behavior alone.[16]

Most of us can agree that it is worthwhile to study behavior, but many people object both to the *a priori* assumption that behavior is all there is to man and to the idea that if mental states do exist, they automatically reveal

24

themselves through overt actions. Surely it is possible to feel deeply, hope intensely, believe fervently, think creatively, or experience other mental activities which are overtly unexpressed and which even the most sophisticated experimental measuring devices cannot detect. Of course the behaviorist might respond that it is also an *a priori* assumption to believe in the existence of mental states and to accept the conclusion that some inner ideas are never expressed in overt behavior or can never be detected by sensitive measuring instruments. The debate then becomes a consideration of which philosophical position, behaviorism or some nonbehavioristic alternative, is supported by the most convincing evidence.

If one chooses the behavioristic position, however, another philosophical problem arises, for if inner thoughts and ideas are only "fictional" (to use Skinner's term), then the thoughts and ideas that form the viewpoint of behaviorism must be fictional too. The theoretical tenets of behaviorism cannot be publicly observed as behavior. So, according to behavioristic theory, these tenets must be dismissed as nonexistent. The theory, therefore, argues itself out of existence.

Closely related to this is the criticism that behaviorism is built on an untenable philosophical base. As we indicated earlier in this chapter, the logical positivism on which modern behaviorism is constructed maintains that anything that cannot be tested experimentally has to be rejected as meaningless and of no value. Regretfully for the positivists, their own theory is not scientifically testable and thus it too must be rejected. Modern behaviorism, therefore, is resting on an untenable philosophical undergirding. With the underlying assumptions knocked out, the behavioristic superstructure must either collapse or be reconstructed on some more stable foundation.

A further philosophical criticism arises in response to the behaviorist assumption that all of the knowledge we have about people, including ourselves, comes through

25   observations of behavior. Undoubtedly we learn about
other people by watching them, but that may not be the
only source of knowledge and it certainly is not how we
usually get knowledge about ourselves. We don't
observe our own bodies, for example, and then conclude
that we are excited, tired, angry, or searching for
something.

> If you see someone rummaging about in the papers
> on his desk, and remember that when he had done
> this on previous occasions the rummaging had
> come to an end when he grabbed hold of his
> spectacles, you might reasonably conclude on these
> grounds that he is now looking for his spectacles.
> But it would be weird if he were to reason as
> follows: "Here I am rummaging about on my desk.
> When I have done this in the past my activity has
> terminated when I have caught hold of my
> spectacles. Therefore, I am probably looking for my
> spectacles!" If you heard a man make such a
> remark and believed that he was not joking, you
> would thereafter regard him with suspicion,
> because of the craziness of the remark.[17]

Behaviorism makes the assumption that human beings
are objects who observe their own outward behavior or
inner physical states and then decide, on the basis of this
self-observation, how they feel or what they think. But is
this how people really behave? Do we always look upon
ourselves solely as an object to be discovered, or is there
something subjective about human nature; something
about our intentions, emotions, or ideas that no outsider
can check and that can never be detected by objective
observation?[18]
    A different kind of philosophical criticism, this one
dealing with ethics, has been raised by Skinner
himself.[19] When someone does something commendable
or praiseworthy he likes to bask in the glory, to receive
the praise of those who commend his creativity or

brilliance, and to accept responsibility for his accomplishments. But when the same person commits a crime or engages in some kind of immoral behavior he is quick to disclaim personal responsibility and to blame his actions on temporary insanity, environmental pressures, a bad upbringing, or some other influence over which he had no control. It may be comfortable for an individual to accept praise for his successes while at the same time disclaiming responsibility for his failures, but it is also inconsistent, as Skinner is honest enough to admit. If all behavior is determined solely by reinforcement, as the behaviorist maintains, then individuals have no responsibility for their failures, but neither can they claim any credit for their successes. This is an inescapable conclusion from behaviorism, but, understandably, for many it is a difficult conclusion to accept.

In addition to these philosophical challenges, behaviorism faces *criticism from physics*. At the beginning of the twentieth century, physics was firmly committed to a view of the universe that had been developed many years previously by Sir Isaac Newton. Newtonian physics claimed that the world was completely orderly and that all events in time and space occurred in accordance with rigid natural laws. Every event was thought to have a prior cause and it was widely agreed that future events could be predicted once the universal laws were discovered. The theory assumed, further, that everything could be measured or quantified, and that all scientific observations could be made with complete objectivity.

This was a concise and convincing theory which experimental psychology accepted without question. Many people felt uncomfortable with the idea that human behavior, like all other events, was determined in accordance with unchanging natural laws, but this seemed to be a conclusion that one had to accept if psychology was to be scientific. That human behavior is orderly, wrote Skinner, is "a working assumption which must be adopted at the very start. We cannot apply the methods of science to a subject matter which is assumed to move about capriciously."[20]

But while the early behaviorists were trying to build psychology on Newtonian physics, the physicists were concluding that Newton was wrong. The new quantum physics had demonstrated that matter moves in an indeterminate or random fashion. There are no rigid natural laws and no invariable cause-effect relationships. Through the use of statistics, we can compute the probability of certain events taking place, but nothing can be predicted with complete certainty. It is not even possible, the new physics concluded, to observe the world with complete objectivity.[21]

Such a conclusion could have had a disturbing influence on experimental psychology, but apparently few psychologists realized the full implications of the new quantum physics. Now it appears that the indeterminacy principle in physics may be less of a threat to psychology than one might have originally supposed. According to Stanford physicist Richard H. Bube, it is possible that indeterminacy is not so much a valid description of reality as an observation that results from imperfect scientific procedures. But even if we assume that the observations are accurate, it must be recognized that indeterminacy is important only for atomic particles. According to Bube, "the mass of a nerve cell, such as might be expected to play a key role in psychological processes in the brain, is some 10^{18} times greater than that of an electron. The direct effects of physical indeterminacy on the nerve cell, therefore, should be negligible."[22] Bube suggests that behavior can be described at many levels, and it does not follow that all levels must be deterministic or indeterministic.[23] It is possible that the behavior of a molecule might be indeterministic while the behavior of a pigeon in a Skinner box might be deterministic. Certainly none of this proves the behavioristic assumption of determinism but it does say that quantum physics might not be so devastating to

28

psychological determinism as some psychologists had feared.

It is not so easy to dismiss another of the challenges that comes from physics, the charge that completely objective observation is impossible. This conclusion is supported even by psychological research evidence.[24] Further, the findings of quantum physics have decisively criticized the experimental psychologist's belief in operationism. Later in his life Bridgman himself concluded that operational definitions were impossible, and other writers have argued that operationism was an obstacle rather than an aid to scientific advance.[25] It has been shown that operationism suffered from the problem of infinite regress (the words used in the operational definition must each be defined operationally; then the words in the second definition must be defined; and so on). Critics claimed that few terms had been or could be operationally defined, and others said that operational definitions were meaningless. The statement that "intelligence is what an intelligence test measures," for example, doesn't tell us much about anything.

All of this has left behavioristic psychology in the awkward position of standing on physical and philosophical foundations that physicists and philosophers have abandoned. Experimental psychologists, intent on collecting data and building their science, apparently have become victims of a selective perception which lets them ignore or forget what is going on in physics and philosophy.

These criticisms of behavioristic experimental psychology have been supplemented by *objections from within psychology* itself. William MacDougall once observed that no behaviorist could ever explain what happens at a symphony concert when "a man...scraping the guts of a cat with hairs from the tail of a horse can produce rapt attention followed by wild applause."

In a more serious vein some psychologists have charged that experimental methods are so artificial that they lead to meaningless results. In attempting to

29   control, manipulate, and measure people in order to
make statements about humanity, experimenters have
been accused of putting subjects into situations where they
behave as little like humans as possible.[26] As a result,
psychological experiments often lead to insignificant
conclusions about unimportant fragments of behavior.

Others have criticized positivism and behaviorism in
general, and Skinner in particular, for concluding that
description is the same as explanation. If we limit
psychology to statements about what we observe and
can describe, this argument states, then we aren't able to
say much about human behavior. As one philosopher
has noted, to assume that description and explanation are
the same is tantamount to eliminating explanation
altogether.[27] Further, if our science can tell us only what
happens but not why, then we cannot even accept the
statement that "description is the same as explanation."
This conclusion itself is not based on a description of
anything observable. It is a presupposition which a
descriptive psychology would have to reject.[28]

Less complicated, perhaps, are charges that
behavioristic psychology tends to make sweeping
conclusions about human beings on the basis of very
limited experimental data.[29] Others complain that by
limiting their study to S-R relationships, by proclaiming
that all explanatory variables "lie outside the organism,"
or by dismissing as irrelevant all that cannot be measured
and controlled, the strict behaviorists prevent
themselves from studying such important human states as
enthusiasm, sexual feelings, surprise, or religious
experience.[30] Some critics argue that the experimental
analysis of behavior leads to conclusions contrary to all
experience and just plain wrong.[31]

Today, as in the past, many psychologists are asking
themselves whether their experimental activities have been
or can be productive. There is a new willingness to
question the previously unquestioned belief that
experimental research is the royal road to knowledge
and a panacea for human problems. Students, impatient to

30

find answers to the pressing problems of society, are turning away from science and are trying to find solutions elsewhere. Some of their professors are claiming that the time has come for psychology to stop trying to imitate natural science and instead to develop some bold new techniques for studying human beings.[32]

But what about Skinner and the hundreds of experimental researchers who still accept behaviorist assumptions? In spite of all the criticisms, these researchers have made significant contributions to our understanding of human behavior.[33] They have struggled to make psychology scientific and they are understandably reluctant to toss aside methods that have been so carefully developed for almost a century.

Experimental psychology must recognize, however, that these methods have limited value and the assumptions on which they are built have questionable validity. It is true that behaviorism has generated research, but, to quote Koch, "those who would argue that the behaviorisms (classical behaviorism and the various forms of neo-behaviorism) have nevertheless been richly productive of research should be reminded that research is not knowledge."[34] Even Skinner, competent scientific technician that he is, has had to go beyond his own data and into the realms of philosophy and political theorizing in order to reach his controversial conclusions about society and human nature. By itself, therefore, behavioristic experimental psychology is inadequate to explain human behavior in all of its richness or to guide psychology toward its stated goal of promoting human welfare.

Footnotes
Chapter 2

[1]Keller, Fred S. *The Definition of Psychology.* New York: Appleton-Century-Crofts, 1937.

[2]Watson, John B. "Psychology as the Behaviorist Views it," *Psychological Review* **20,** 1913, pp. 158-177. This was the first official statement of behaviorism, a statement that caused considerable stir in academic circles when it was first published.

[3]Koch, Sigmund. "Psychology and Emerging Conceptions of Knowledge as Unity." In T. W. Wann (ed.), *Behaviorism and Phenomenology.*

31

Chicago: University of Chicago Press, 1964, pp. 1-41. See also Professor Koch's article on behaviorism in *Encyclopedia Brittanica,* 1971, vol. 3, pp. 398-403.

[4]*Encyclopedia Britannica,* 1971, vol. 14, pp. 237-9.

[5]Stevens, S. S. "The Operational Basis of Psychology," *American Journal of Psychology* **47,** 1935, pp. 517-527. Quoted in Plutchik, Robert, "Operation as Methodology," *Behavioral Science* **8,** 1963, pp. 234-241.

[6]The weakness of operationism has been described in several places including the article by Plutchik, *ibid.*

[7]Walker, Edward L. "Relevant Psychology Is a Snark," *American Psychologist* **25,** 1970, pp. 1081-1086; Baron, Jonathan, "Is Experimental Psychology Relevant?" *American Psychologist* **26,** 1971, pp. 713-716.

[8]Thomson, Robert. *The Pelican History of Psychology.* Baltimore: Penguin, 1968, p. 430.

[9]Koch, *op. cit.,* pp. 20, 21.

[10]The papers presented at the conference and a summary of the discussions that followed are given in Wann, *op. cit.*

[11]Wann, *op. cit.,* p. 106.

[12]Skinner, B. F. *Beyond Freedom and Dignity.* New York: Alfred A. Knopf, 1971. See also Skinner, B. F., *Science and Human Behavior.* New York: The Free Press, 1953, pp. 446-449; "Skinner's Utopia: Panacea or Path to Hell?" *Time,* September 20, 1971, pp. 47-53.

[13]Holmes, Arthur F. *Faith Seeks Understanding.* Grand Rapids: Eerdmans, 1971, p. 117.

[14]Matson, Floyd W. (ed.). *Without/Within: Behaviorism and Humanism.* Monterey, California: Brooks/Cole, 1973. See especially the chapters by Kenneth MacCorquodale and Willard F. Day.

[15]Skinner, B. F. *Beyond Freedom and Dignity.* See especially the last chapter.

[16]*Ibid.*

[17]Malcolm, Norman. "Behaviorism as a Philosophy." In Wann, *op. cit.,* p. 151. Writing in Matson, *op. cit.* (p. 30), Willard F. Day argues that such descriptions are a "grotesque parody of behaviorism" but the writer nevertheless sticks with the conclusion that private experience is behavior which is observed by the individual behaver.

[18]Malcolm, *ibid.,* gives a clear discussion of behaviorism's tendency to regard man solely as an object.

[19]Skinner, *Beyond Freedom and Dignity,* chapter 3. This inconsistency is discussed in more detail by Tournier, Paul, *The Person Reborn,* New York: Harper & Row, 1966, chapter 11.

[20]Skinner, B. F. *Science and Human Behavior,* p. 6.

[21]Oppenheimer, Robert. "Analogy in Science," *American Psychologist* **11,** 1956, pp. 127-135; Van Kamm, Adrian, "Assumptions in Psychology," *Journal of Individual Psychology* **14,** 1958, pp. 22-28 (reprinted in Schultz, Duane P., *The Science of Psychology: Critical Reflections,* New York: Appleton-Century-Crofts, 1970, pp. 24-29); Heisenberg, W. *Physics and Philosophy: The Revolution in Modern Physics.* New York: Harper & Row, 1958.

[22]Bube, Richard H. *The Human Quest.* Waco, Texas: Word, 1971, p. 169.

[23]*Ibid.,* pp. 135-6, 168-171.

32

[24]Schultz, *op. cit.* See especially the section on "methodological issues"; Rosenthal, R. *Experimenter Effects in Behavioral Research.* New York: Appleton, 1966.

[25]Bridgman's later conclusions are reported in Matson, Floyd W., *The Broken Image: Man, Science, and Society.* New York: George Braziller, 1964, pp. 249-250. For a concise criticism of operationalism see Plutchik, Robert, "Operation as Methodology," *op. cit.* (reprinted in Schultz, *op. cit.,* pp. 87-97).

[26]Bannister, D. "Psychology as an Exercise in Paradox," *Bulletin of the British Psychological Society* **19,** 1966, pp. 21-26 (reprinted in Schultz, *op. cit.,* pp. 4-10).

[27]Clark, Gordon H. *Religion, Reason, and Revelation.* Nutley, New Jersey: The Craig Press, 1961, pp. 11-12.

[28]*Ibid.*

[29]Holmes, *op. cit.,* p. 14. The charge certainly applies to Skinner who has freely but creatively extended his experimental conclusions about reinforcement contingencies to describe, for example, how we would change our educational system (see *The Technology of Teaching,* New York: Appleton-Century-Crofts, 1968) or how we can alter our whole society (see *Walden Two,* New York: Macmillan, 1949; and *Beyond Freedom and Dignity).*

[30]Hammes, John A. "Beyond Freedom and Dignity: Behavioral Fixated Delusion?" *Journal of Psychology and Theology* **1,** July 1973, pp. 8-14.

[31]See, for example, the much acclaimed review by Noam Chomsky of Skinner's book *Verbal Behavior* ("Review of *Verbal Behavior,* by B. F. Skinner," *Language* **35,** 1959, pp. 26-58). Chomsky concludes that a child simply does not and cannot learn a language in the way that Skinner maintains he does. See also Braginsky, B. M., & Braginsky, D. D., *Mainstream Psychology: A Critique.* New York: Holt, Rinehart and Winston, 1974, chapter 3 "Method and Theory—The Heart of Behaviorism."

[32]Bakan, David. "Psychology Can Now Kick the Science Habit," *Psychology Today* **5,** March 1972, pp. 26, 28, 86-88.

[33]Among those who deny Skinner's contribution are Braginsky & Braginsky, *op. cit.,* who after a careful review of behaviorist methodology, make the following statement: "An analysis of Skinnerian thought will indicate that the criticisms and alarm Skinner has aroused are unwarranted. There can be few ramifications of his work since Skinner's contributions to the knowledge of psychology have been minimal" (pp. 62-3).

[34]Koch, Sigmund. "Psychology Cannot be a Coherent Science," *Psychology Today* **3,** September 1969, p. 66.

Chapter Three

PSYCHOLOGY IN THE CONSULTING ROOM

WHILE Wundt and his students were busy with the laboratory research that helped to establish psychology as an independent science, another movement was beginning in a different part of Europe. Far removed from psychological laboratories and academic classrooms, Dr. Sigmund Freud of Vienna was being consulted by emotionally disturbed people who wanted relief from their tensions. As he listened to these patients and observed their symptoms, the young Dr. Freud began to formulate a set of theories which, in the years that followed, led to heated debate and gave rise to a movement that even today challenges the foundations of academic experimental psychology.

Freud, like Wundt, was a physician who had a strong interest in physiology but little desire to practice general medicine. Beyond this, however, the founding fathers of experimental and clinical psychology had almost nothing in common. Wundt worked in a university, surrounded by bright and admiring young students, all of whom were using the experimental method to study conscious awareness. In contrast, Freud worked alone, at least in the beginning, using clinical interviews in an attempt to uncover what he called the "unconscious" causes of behavior. The Psychiatric and Neurological Society of Vienna gave his ideas a cool reception, his early books attracted little attention, and it was not until 1909, when Freud was fifty-three, that he was first invited to present his theories in a university lecture. He was often criticized and ridiculed because of his views (in 1933 the Nazis burned his books, along with others, in a public bonfire). Although suffering from cancer (he had thirty-three operations during the last fifteen years of his life), Freud nevertheless continued to develop the controversial theories which one writer has called "by far the most important contributions that have been made to human psychology to date."[1] Even those who reject the tenets of psychoanalysis agree that Freud's influence on twentieth-century psychology has been profound.[2]

36   Freud was an astute observer of behavior, a creative
thinker, and a prolific writer.[3] During his lifetime he was
constantly revising the details of his theories, but
psychoanalysis always rested on two fundamental
hypotheses.[4] The first of these was the principle of
psychic determinism: the view that all behavior is caused.
Freud believed that none of our mental activities could
happen by chance or in a random way. All thoughts and
dreams, all behavior, all of the things we forget, all
mistakes and slips of the tongue have a prior cause. But the
causes of behavior are often difficult to identify because
they are frequently unconscious. This brings us to the
second fundamental hypothesis: most behavior results
from the influence of "unconscious mental processes."
Freud would never have felt comfortable in the
psychological laboratories where researchers were
studying conscious awareness. He believed that the
conscious part of the mind accounted for very few of our
actions. To understand behavior it was necessary to
uncover the unconscious causes, and this was what the
methods of psychoanalysis were designed to do.

It is well known that Freud's conclusions were
controversial, so much so that even his closest associates
criticized the master and set up competing psychological
systems of their own. Most of the critics felt that Freud
had placed too much emphasis on sex. Others disagreed
with his rigid determinism and unwillingness to
acknowledge free will, his overemphasis on the
importance of childhood experiences, his ignoring of
social influences on behavior, or his tendency to observe a
relatively few neurotic people and from this to make
sweeping generalizations about the human race.
Experimentally-oriented psychologists were among
those who argued that concepts such as the *id, psychic
energy,* or *penis envy* were figments of Freud's
imagination and impossible for independent observers to
see. Even more amazing to non-Freudians were some of
the psychoanalytic explanations of specific human actions.
That paranoid suspicion of others is associated with

37

homosexuality, or that painters and pottery-makers often have an unconscious desire to play with human excreta, are conclusions that fit psychoanalytic theory but were rejected as pure fantasy by nonbelievers.[5] So complete was the system, however, that even the attacks of critics and their "resistance" to the theory could be explained away psychoanalytically. It must have seemed to many people that Freud had developed a system that could neither be proven by accepted scientific methods nor attacked in a way that Freudians would accept.

In spite of the theory's weaknesses, many of Freud's conclusions have been widely accepted into psychology. His emphasis on the importance of early childhood, for example, his views of defense mechanisms (especially as they were developed by Anna Freud, his daughter), and even his belief in the unconscious determinants of behavior are generally included as a valid part of contemporary psychology.

But perhaps Freud's greatest contribution was to serve as a catalyst whose ideas led to a burst of creative thinking. Psychoanalysis provided stimulation for the development of new theories and the finding of better ways to understand and help people. Alfred Adler, the first of Freud's associates to break away, played down the unconscious, stressed the importance of social influences on behavior, first suggested the notion of "inferiority complex," and decided that face-to-face counseling was better than using a couch. Carl Jung, another deserter, rejected Freud's views on sex, expanded the idea of the unconscious, developed thoughtful ideas about extroversion and introversion, wrote about the social masks or "persona" that people wear to protect themselves in public, and extended his psychology to consider folklore, myth, and religious symbolism. In the 1920s, Otto Rank, who had been Freud's protégé and one of his closest friends, accidentally fell out of the master's favor by proposing that birth was a universally traumatic experience and by suggesting that the will was an important determinant of behavior.

38   With the notable exception of Rank, most of the early
Freudians had been trained in medicine and were
involved in the practice of psychiatry. Freud himself did
not believe that medical training was necessary for a
psychotherapist (a conclusion with which many
contemporary psychiatrists would disagree),[6] so the
post-Freudian schools of analysis attracted the attention
of many laypeople. Rank, for example, was widely
recognized as the father of American social work, a
mental health field that has grown in significance even
though it is outside the medical profession.

Beginning psychology students often assume that
Freud and his psychoanalytic ideas form a major part of
modern psychology, but this is not true. Around the time
of the first world war, when Freud's theories were having
their greatest impact, academic psychologists were
basking in the discovery of behaviorism. Psychology was
at last beginning to look like a science, and few people
in the universities wanted to accept something as vague
and seemingly nonscientific as psychoanalysis. The
various clinical outgrowths of Freudianism, some of
which bore almost no resemblance to the system from
which they had come, found little acceptance in academic
ivory towers. Thus in the words of one historian, clinical
psychology had to go underground.

In virtually every introductory course in psychology,
there was war between experimental (academic)
and underground (clinical) psychology.
Behavioristically-minded professors sought to
convert their underground-informed students, to
exorcise heresies from their minds. Students who
wanted good grades, admission to graduate school
and, ultimately, faculty appointments, managed to
adjure the errors of their youth and become true
believers. Heretics rarely made it to graduate
school.[7]

39

The relatively few clinical psychologists who broke the barrier and permeated academic circles were looked down upon by the experimentalists who felt that their domain had been invaded by pseudoscientists.

Then came World War II. Soldiers and veterans needed help and the United States government expressed willingness to finance clinical training. This put the psychology departments in a difficult position. Should they refuse the offered money and remain rigidly experimental, or should they accept it and expand their clinical training programs? Many universities took the latter course, but clinical faculty and students were still scorned by experimentalists who tended to have little respect for the newcomers. As a postwar field of study, psychology took a great leap forward. But it was a divided psychology, split into two opposing factions which, in spite of frequent gestures toward rapproachement, have maintained their separation right down to the present.[8]

It would be wrong for anyone to assume, however, that clinical psychology has limped along as a purely speculative discipline that is little more than an unproductive embarrassment for the more rigorous experimentalists. On the contrary, it could be argued that clinicians have accomplished as much as or even more than experimental psychology. The development and perfection of psychological tests is perhaps the most unique accomplishment, but clinicians have played significant roles in the study of such diverse issues as child development, social deviance, interpersonal relations, prejudice, mental retardation, the nature of personality, individual differences, attitude change, the influence of drugs, and the process of aging. Clinical psychologists have also developed a number of widely used counseling techniques, and the field of clinical psychology, more than any other group among the mental health professions, has shown itself willing to examine critically its own treatment procedures.[9]

Clinicians have never had any overarching philosophy like behaviorism to provide a central rallying point for

40   their branch of psychology; neither has clinical
psychology had a Watson or a Skinner to give the field a
unified sense of direction. Second to Freud, the most
influential clinician has probably been Carl Rogers. He
rejected Freud's pessimistic view of the human race,
Skinner's conception of man as a responding organism,
and the rigid determinism of both psychoanalysis and
behaviorism. In place of this, Rogers has maintained that
man is innately good, unique, creative, and free to
develop his own destiny. When he proposed his
client-centered or nondirective technique of therapy in the
1940s, Rogers was among the first to assert that there
must be a warm personal relationship between the
therapist and his counselee if therapy is to be successful.
Following the second world war, when group counseling
came into prominence, Rogers was a leader in the field
and even today he is one of the most articulate advocates
of the encounter-group experience. Rogers considers
himself a scientist, however, and in this role has made what
is undoubtedly one of his most significant contributions:
the demonstration that therapy can be studied objectively
and scientifically. Rogers' many original contributions to
both psychological practice and research have done much
to establish clinical psychology as an authentic scientific
discipline and a respectable mental health profession.

Nevertheless, like experimental behaviorism, clinical
psychology is under attack. In the words of one of its
leaders, clinical psychology has had a "short, unhappy
life" and is facing an "uncertain future."[10] Although a
number of weaknesses have been identified, clinical
psychology appears to suffer from four major problems:
crisis in identity, excessive diversity, questionable
effectiveness, and persisting determinism.

The *crisis in identity* has been discussed most clearly in
George Albee's controversial presidential address.[11]
Among other problems, the clinical psychologist is
confused about his role and his function; he does not

41   know how to answer the questions, "Who am I?" and
"What am I supposed to be doing?"

Most clinical psychologists work in universities or
psychiatric treatment centers and in both locations the
clinician frequently feels like a second-class citizen.
Previously we noted the reluctance of experimental
psychologists to embrace their clinical colleagues
because of a suspicion that "applied psychology" is in
some way less scientific or less academically respectable
than laboratory research. Even in those universities
where clinicians do enjoy a reputable status, they often
harbor a vague feeling that graduate departments of
psychology may not be the best places for training
counselors in professional skills. But what is the
alternative? The psychiatric settings which employ so
many clinical psychologists offer even less acceptance.
Many psychiatrists look down on psychologists because of
their lack of medical knowledge, so there is frequently
an unwillingness to accept a clinician as a competent
therapist or an equal partner on the treatment team. The
psychologist who remains in the psychiatric setting feels
pressure to accept the so-called "sickness model" which
assumes that "mental illness" is a disease to be diagnosed
and treated—presumably by a medical doctor. Both in
the university and in the treatment center, therefore, the
young psychologist begins to wonder, "Why am I here
and what am I supposed to be doing?"

A partial answer to these questions was provided
several years ago at a conference in Boulder, Colorado,
with a proposal that clinical psychologists must be both
scientists trained to do empirical research and
professional counselors competent to help people with
their problems.[12] Undoubtedly there is merit in this
suggestion. The scientist-professional model has
stimulated creative clinical research and given a clear
direction to many training programs. But many
clinicians aren't interested in being researchers. Graduate
students who want to help troubled people solve their
problems are frustrated when their training requires an

42

empirical research thesis and a knowledge of such nonclinical matters as experimental design, statistics, or factor analysis. It has even been suggested that the roles of scientist and professional are mutually incompatible. The professional counselor exists to serve society, change people's behavior, relate to others in close interpersonal contact, and keep quiet about confidential matters. In contrast, the researcher seeks to gain scientific knowledge. He may hope that his work will have practical relevance some day, but it isn't his task to reform the people who are subjects in his experiments. He strives to remain objective and he abhors secrecy or the withholding of facts uncovered in his work.

Other professions have also had to carve out an image for themselves and find a unique place of service, but never before have professions become so large while the professional image was so unclear. Freud had the problem of molding his theory of psychoanalysis and persuading others of its value, but the early analysts were a small group and most were securely grounded in medicine. Other professions, such as nursing, developed a clear image and area of service before growing in numbers. In contrast, there are already more than 10,000 clinical psychologists in the United States and their numbers are increasing by 500 Ph.D.s a year—more than in physiological, comparative, and experimental psychology combined.[13] Creative, capable people[14] are actively involved in developing and improving clinical psychology, but progress in their profession seems slow; members of the guild lack a clear sense of identity and often feel at least a touch of professional inferiority.

It is not surprising that clinical psychology has split into an *excessive diversity* of theories, techniques, and opinions. Consider, for example, the forms of psychotherapy that have been proposed, often with evangelistic optimism and zeal, by people who sometimes are critical of all competing methods. Existential therapy and the logotherapy of Frankl assert that the counselee must be helped to develop values and find

43 meaning in life. The client-centered theory that Rogers developed seeks to support "clients" as they explore feelings and develop a more positive self-image. In contrast, directive approaches assume that the counselor must take primary responsibility for changing the counselee's behavior. Mowrer's integrity therapy encourages people to make confessions and atone for guilt-producing actions. The rational-emotive therapy of Ellis asserts that undesirable beliefs, illogical ideas, and self-defeating thoughts are harmful and must deliberately be eliminated. The learning or behavior therapies assume that change comes only when the scientifically discovered principles of learning are applied in a way that eliminates the harmful training of the past and teaches new ways for behaving in the future. The list could go on—Gestalt therapy, hypnotherapy, transactional analysis, primal therapy, psychodrama, radical therapy, general semantics therapy—each differs from all others and sometimes the systems are diametrically opposed to one another. Glasser's reality therapy, for example, is in many respects the opposite of psychoanalysis. Reality therapy advocates active dialogue, genuine friendship between the therapist and his patient, de-emphasis on childhood experiences or events of the past, ignoring of the unconscious, relative disinterest in feelings or motives, emphasis on the moral "right or wrong" of behavior, and frank consideration of practical ways for people to become more responsible in their actions and realistic in their thinking.[15] Freud would have considered all of this to be heresy. Further, Glasser's assertion that it would take only one day to teach a bright young trainee all he needs to know about therapy[16] would be enough to make the founder of psychoanalysis turn over in his grave.

Many of the new therapeutic techniques have originated with psychologists, but other professions have contributed to the diversity. Glasser, for example, is a psychiatrist, but his methods, like most other nonmedical procedures, have found their way into the treatment

44 repertoire of at least some clinical psychologists.

It could be argued that this diversity is a good thing, a sign that clinical psychology is alive, healthy, productive, and creative. It has been estimated, however, that there are now over 200 different schools of therapy having roughly 10,000 specific techniques.[17] Rather than reflecting professional competence and productivity, such a proliferation of methods could be seen as a monument to the confusion or inefficiency of clinicians, a demonstration that therapists really don't know what they're doing. Medical historian F. H. Garrison commented on this subject years ago. "Whenever many different remedies are used for a disease," he wrote, "it usually means that we know very little about the disease,"[18] or, perhaps, about effective treatment.

This brings us to a third major problem with clinical psychology, its *questionable effectiveness*. Using a variety of techniques and measuring devices (including questionnaires, rating scales, personality tests, interviews, physiological measurements, analyses of tape recordings or films of therapy, and studies of laboratory analogues of treatment), numerous researchers have attempted to discover whether or not clinical methods really work. The number of studies in this area is impressive,[19] but the research findings are not encouraging. After surveying much of the literature, for example, Eysenck[20] concluded that the studies all reached the same conclusion: therapy does not work very well. Researchers on both sides of the Atlantic, studying adults as well as children, discovered that experienced therapists are not much better than the inexperienced; that untreated people recover at about the same rate as those in treatment; and that all types of counseling are equally ineffective, except possibly the learning and group therapies which are slightly better than the others.[21]

These conclusions raised a storm of protest, especially from psychotherapists whose livelihood depended on the effectiveness of their treatment techniques and whose personal experiences contradicted the research findings

45   that Eysenck had summarized. Some argued that the evidence was ambiguous and could be interpreted in different ways; others expressed the opinion that empirical research could never lead to an effective appraisal of the value of psychotherapy.

Certainly the researcher encounters some formidable obstacles in this kind of work. He has difficulty, for example, in measuring variables like "improvement" or "effectiveness of therapy" and it is even harder to determine with accuracy exactly what the therapist is doing in his work. Counselors and patients are understandably reluctant to cooperate in research, lest the investigators interfere with the effectiveness of treatment, although "the patient's welfare" sometimes becomes an excuse that therapists use in order to cover their own insecurity about being carefully studied or having their effectiveness challenged. It is easy to sympathize with this attitude, but in so doing we can also applaud both those who have been courageous enough to let their work be examined and those who have attempted to investigate the therapeutic process.

The investigations, however, have not given clinicians much cause for encouragement. While it is generally agreed that Eysenck's early conclusions were overly pessimistic, there is still not a lot of evidence to support the effectiveness of therapy. After reviewing 214 studies and research summaries, for example, Bergin concluded that

> ...our comprehensive view of the literature must be considered more favorable than that of Eysenck's 1966 survey, although we certainly cannot point to more than a moderately positive, average therapeutic effect.... There remains only some modest evidence that psychotherapy "works." While most studies do not seem to yield very substantial evidence that this is so, the number that do seems to be clearly larger than would be expected by chance.[22]

46   Such a statement is hardly a rousing cheer in favor of therapy's effectiveness. As Bergin and others have pointed out, the averaging of data hides the fact that while perhaps two-thirds of all therapists are ineffective or even harmful, at least a minority are very capable indeed.[23] But the success of this minority apparently has little to do with their training, theoretical orientation, or methodology. More important than any of these are the counselor's warmth, genuine concern for people, and sensitivity to the counselee's feelings and needs. [24] Therapeutic techniques may be important but it appears that they are less significant than the counselor's self-confidence, the counselee's expectation that he will recover, and the nature of the relationship between therapist and client.[25]

If these conclusions are true, why do so many people ignore them and go on believing in the value of therapy? Perhaps many of us find it too painful or threatening to acknowledge that psychology might not work, so we assume that our personal experience contradicts the scientific findings. Research shows that many people, perhaps 30 percent of those in need of treatment, improve spontaneously.[26] If one is seeing a therapist during this time of improvement and paying money, it is natural to assume that the improvement is *caused* by the expensive treatment, even though the treatment and the improvement may have nothing to do with each other. Further, as we have already seen, a few clinicians are highly effective. The notable success of these practitioners could lead some of us to dismiss the unwelcome scientific studies by proclaiming that empirical research techniques simply can not appraise the value of clinical procedures.

As a graduate student, I took a course in Rorschach testing. Students in the class read many articles showing that the test was of no value, but our professor demonstrated that by listening to a few Rorschach responses he could draw conclusions which in a remarkable way paralleled other information that was available about the patient. Most of us decided that our

47 live professor was more to be trusted than dead research reports. It may be that clinical psychology needs new and more powerful research techniques to prove its worth, but until these are forthcoming we must use methods that are available. Regretfully, these have not been complimentary about the value of therapeutic procedures.

Techniques of therapy are not the only clinical methods to come under attack. The techniques of research that clinicians use have also been criticized. Freud, for example, built conclusions on the verbatim reports of a comparatively few people, most of whom were neurotic. He assumed that his patients were telling the truth and accepted their reports at face value. Freud usually recorded his data after the interview, working on the questionable assumption that he would remember what was important. His observations could not be verified or repeated by others, he was never able to predict behavior, and he never used control groups or other devices to check the accuracy of his observations. It is hardly surprising, therefore, that Freud was criticized as an exceptionally biased researcher who saw only what he wanted to see and who read into his cases the conclusions he wanted to find.[27]

Modern clinical researchers are, for the most part, much more sophisticated, but there is still a tendency to observe relatively few subjects and to base conclusions on skimpy "case history" evidence. Replication of clinical findings is so difficult that it is rarely done, and clinical investigators often study emotionally disturbed subjects who are not representative samples of the population. It might be argued that the problems studied by clinicians are more complex than those of the experimental psychologist. The clinician finds it more difficult to control variables or to make precise measurements. He often sees no alternative to the case study or "naturalistic observation methods" even though he realizes that these are among the least accurate of research techniques. Many clinicians are doing what they can with the best techniques available, and others are trying to find new methods with which to evaluate their techniques. Until research shows otherwise, however, clinicians must consider the possibility that the methods of clinical psychology and the techniques of modern psychotherapy are of questionable validity.

The *determinism* and mechanistic view of man, which characterize experimental psychology, are less rigidly held by clinicians. Freud, of course, was a strong believer in determinism and postulated that the causes of behavior were hidden in the unconscious where they are difficult to observe or understand. Modern learning therapists have built their therapy on deterministic, behavioristic assumptions, but many other clinicians refuse to view human beings as robots with behavior that is completely determined. People are seen, instead, as persons who have significance, worth, and individual freedom.[28]

To accept such a view, however, seems to reject the Newtonian model on which psychology is built, and some clinicians, like their experimental colleagues, are unable to do this. They prefer to try to accept both positions and to believe in both freedom and psychological determinism. Other clinical psychologists who overlook philosophical issues are not rigidly bound to behaviorist methodology. They do not feel compelled to accept the outmoded positivistic philosophy on which experimental psychology is built. A clinical psychologist accepts the empirical method, but he may also admit that difficult-to-observe things like hope, meaning, values, motives, or goals do exist and do influence behavior.

In spite of this more flexible approach, many clinicians recognize that all is not well in their profession. Committed clinical psychologists may find satisfaction in their work, but they know that many of their colleagues, especially in experimental psychology and psychiatry, look down on them and question their ability to make useful contributions to the betterment of society.

49   They know that their research methods aren't very good, that many consider their skills to be of questionable value, and that fellow clinicians are suggesting publicly that their field has an "uncertain future." Perhaps clinical psychology, like experimental psychology, is failing to explain behavior and is doing very little to help people function more effectively.

Footnotes
Chapter 3

[1]Brenner, Charles. *An Elementary Textbook of Psychoanalysis.* Garden City, New York: Doubleday, 1957, p. 1.

[2]In a survey of 1,000 American psychologists, Skinner was chosen as the most important figure in contemporary psychology, while Freud was selected as the man who has had the greatest influence on psychology in the twentieth century. See Wright, G. D., "A Further Note on Ranking the Important Psychologists," *American Psychologist* **25,** 1970, pp. 650-651.

[3]See Brenner, *op. cit.,* or Hall, C. S., *A Primer of Freudian Psychology.* New York: A Mentor Book, 1954. A shorter but excellent summary of psychoanalysis is found in Hall, C. S. and Lindzey, G., *Theories of Personality* (2nd ed.). New York: Wiley, 1970.

[4]Brenner, *op. cit.,* chapter 1.

[5]For a concise summary of psychoanalytic tenets which psychiatry cannot accept, see Arieti, Silvano, "The Present Status of Psychiatric Theory," *American Journal of Psychiatry* **124:**12, June 1968, pp. 1630-1639.

[6]Freud stated his belief in *The Question of Lay Analysis,* New York: Norton, 1950 (1926). In contrast, notice the following statement in Brenner, *op. cit.,* p. 6: "It is obvious to us today that the more thorough a physician's medical training, the better his therapeutic results."

[7]Bakan, David. "Psychology Can Now Kick the Science Habit," *Psychology Today,* March 1972, p. 86.

[8]This division is one of the major issues discussed in the presidential address of Albee, George W., "The Uncertain Future of Clinical Psychology," *American Psychologist* **25,** 1970, pp. 1071-1080.

[9]See, for example, Strupp, H. H., Fox, R. E., and Lessler, K., *Patients View Their Psychotherapy,* Baltimore: Johns-Hopkins, 1969; Bergin, Allen E. and Garfield, Sol L. (ed.), *Handbook of Psychotherapy and Behavior Change,* New York: Wiley, 1971; or Eysenck, H. J., "The Effects of Psychotherapy." In Eysenck, H. J. (ed.), *Handbook of Abnormal Psychology,* New York: Basic Books, 1961, pp. 697-725.

[10]Albee, *op. cit.,* and Albee, G. W., "The Short, Unhappy Life of Clinical Psychology," *Psychology Today* **4,** September 1970, pp. 42-3, 74-5.

[11]*Ibid.*

[12]Raimy, V. C. (ed.). *Training in Clinical Psychology* (The Boulder Conference Report). New York: Prentice-Hall, 1950.

[13]Albee, *op. cit.,* pp. 1078, 1080.

[14]A report by the National Council of Graduate Departments of Psychology notes that "getting into graduate school in psychology may be harder than getting into medical school." The people who do get accepted are among the brightest of applicants but these creative people often feel a confusion over their identity as they move into the job market. "Students at all levels are discovering that they have been duped," the report continues. "Clinical psychology is not the promised land of unlimited...jobs and opportunities.... In our attempts to sell our science-profession and its training programs we have oversold ourselves and now have too many applicants for too few training slots, too many graduates for too few jobs." See "Report Finds Psychology 'Oversold' to Graduate Students," APA Monitor 4, July 1973, pp. 1, 4.

[15]Glasser, William. Reality Therapy. New York: Harper & Row, 1965.

[16]Havermann, Ernest. "Alternatives to Analysis," Playboy, November 1969, p. 214.

[17]Ibid., p. 134.

[18]Garrison, F. H. An Introduction to the History of Medicine. Philadelphia: Saunders, 1921. Quoted in Bergin and Garfield, op. cit., p. 463.

[19]Bergin and Garfield's edited volume, op. cit., for example, contains over 900 pages and summarizes literally hundreds of studies on the effectiveness of psychotherapy and behavior change.

[20]Eysenck, op cit. See also Eysenck, H. J., The Effects of Psychotherapy, New York: International Science Press, 1966.

[21]See Paul, G. L., Insight vs. Desensitization in Psychotherapy, Stanford: Stanford University Press, 1966; and Rogers, C. R., Carl Rogers on Encounter Groups, New York: Harper & Row, 1970.

[22]Bergin, Allen E. "The Evaluation of Therapeutic Outcomes." In Bergin and Garfield, op. cit., pp. 217-270. The quotation is from page 229.

[23]Bergin, ibid.; Truax, Charles B. and Mitchell, Kevin H., "Research on Certain Therapist Interpersonal Skills in Relation to Process and Outcome." In Bergin and Garfield, op. cit., p. 337.

[24]Truax and Mitchell, ibid., pp. 310-319.

[25]Coulson, William R. and Rogers, Carl R. (ed.). Man and the Science of Man. Columbus, Ohio: Charles E. Merrill, 1968, p. 197.

[26]Bergin, op. cit., pp. 239-246. The argument in the text may be unfair at this point. Bergin found that spontaneous recovery rates range from 0 to 46 percent. He has raised the possibility that those who improve do so not because of spontaneous change, but because of the "amateur" and informal counseling of friends, relatives, or other concerned individuals.

[27]Hall and Lindzey, op. cit.

[28]See, for example, Rogers, C. R., On Becoming a Person: A Therapist's View of Psychotherapy, Boston: Houghton-Mifflin, 1961: Wilson, Colin, New Pathways in Psychology, London: Victor Gollancz, 1972; and Chein, Isidor, The Science of Behavior and the Image of Man, New York: Basic Books, 1972.

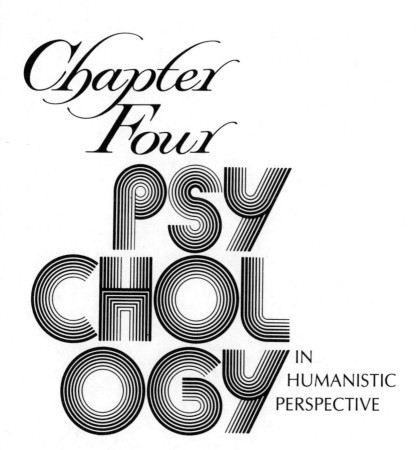

Chapter Four

PSYCHOLOGY IN HUMANISTIC PERSPECTIVE

IN the preceding chapters, an attempt has been made to show that contemporary psychology is growing in popularity, but is struggling with a number of internal problems. Some who are psychologists enthusiastically proclaim that this science has the potential to save society from self-destruction, but to many of us such rhetoric has a hollow ring. Many psychologists feel that the present influence and future potential of psychology is in danger of being weakened because it is divided into at least two opposing factions: the experimental camp with its roots in behaviorism, and the clinical camp which is an outgrowth of psychoanalysis. Within each camp there is even further turmoil and instability. Experimentalists disagree with other experimentalists. Clinicians are divided into a variety of factions and schools of psychotherapy. Some psychologists, therefore, are turning their attention to the problems of their particular science and to its prospects for the future. There is an increasing desire to put our house in order lest we slip into further irrelevancy or ineffectiveness.

Many of psychology's critics have aligned themselves with a new movement, sometimes called humanistic psychology, but more often referred to as "the third force" between behaviorism and psychoanalysis. At the present time, humanistic or third force psychology does not claim to be a new school or system.[1] It is, instead, a growing protest movement that acknowledges the accomplishments of the two major forces in psychology, but seeks to overcome their weaknesses by introducing new goals, new methods, and above all, new respect for the individual as a person.

The basic tenets of the third force movement are perhaps as old as recorded history and many of the leading figures in psychology—Rollo May, Carl Rogers,[2] Gordon Allport, O. Hobart Mowrer, Erich Fromm, for example—showed humanistic leanings in their writing long before the new psychology became popular or identifiable as a separate movement. It was not until the 1960s that "humanistic psychology" became a widely

54   used term. Although the movement could not be said to
have a founder, its chief architect was clearly Abraham H.
Maslow.

As a young man living in New York, Maslow had met
and attended the lectures of such famous people as
Alfred Adler, Erich Fromm, Karen Horney, Kurt Goldstein,
and Ruth Benedict. Maslow was a protégé of both Harry
Harlow and William Sheldon (who wrote about the
correlation between psychological temperament and
physiology) and for a period of time he worked in the
laboratory of E. L. Thorndike, who was one of Watson's
most devoted disciples. These contacts with famous and
capable people undoubtedly gave Maslow a healthy
respect for both behaviorism and psychoanalysis, but he
also saw that the two main forces in psychology had
definite weaknesses. "It is very difficult," he once wrote

> to communicate to others my simultaneous respect
> for and impatience with these two comprehensive
> psychologies. So many people insist on being *either*
> pro-Freudian *or* anti-Freudian, pro-scientific *or*
> anti-scientific psychology, etc. In my opinion all such
> loyalty-positions are silly. Our job is to integrate
> these various truths into the *whole* truth, which
> should be our only loyalty.[3]

With creativity, boldness, and enthusiasm, Maslow set
out to evaluate what was useful and relevant in the
psychologies of his day. He had no desire to be the
founder of a new movement in psychology, nor did he
want to create dissension in the field. Yet in a sense he
did both. Early in his career, Maslow had coauthored a
highly acclaimed textbook on abnormal psychology.
Subsequently he reached the conclusion that psychologists
should also be concerned with the study of healthy,
normal human beings. Soon he was finding and observing
people who were outstanding examples of good mental
health. He developed a creative new listing of human
needs and described how people could, by developing

55 their "unrealized potential," move toward a state of psychological maturity that he called self-actualization. He grappled with the problems of improving mental health, making education more effective, helping neurotics to function more efficiently, and improving society. He was the first person to use the term "third force." As one of the founders of both the American Association for Humanistic Psychology and the *Journal of Humanistic Psychology,* he endowed the new movement with an optimistic belief in the potential and innate goodness of mankind. During his lifetime, Maslow wrote numerous articles and books, rose like Skinner and Rogers to become president of the American Psychological Association, and until his sudden death in 1970 remained at the vanguard of the new humanistic movement.[4]

Third force psychology, like the experimental and clinical traditions from which it comes, is a diversified and complex movement which we will look at from three vantage points: what it opposes, what it affirms or stands for, and what it lists as its major goals.[5]

James F. T. Bugental, one of the most articulate spokespersons for the humanistic position, has written that the new psychology differs from the old in many ways, but lists six issues of special importance.[6] First, the third force movement opposes the idea that we can learn very much about man by studying animals. Such a procedure, Bugental writes, gives an "inadequate and even misleading" description of how human beings function. Second, the humanist resists behavioristic conclusions that psychology can investigate only observable behavior. Instead of restricting his study to overt actions, the humanistic psychologist attempts to study the whole person and boldly considers such hitherto forbidden subjects as hope, ecstasy, love, fear, or expectations. Third, the new movement criticizes psychology's tendency to stick with rigid methodology wrapped up in an outdated logical positivist tradition. The

56   humanists believe that psychological researchers should
be concerned more about studying problems of humanity
and less about whether their experiments are technically
well-designed or scientifically sophisticated. We should
ask "What problems need to be studied?" instead of
trying to think of what experiments can be done with
available techniques. Fourth, the new movement
challenges the "myth" that research always precedes
practical application. Sometimes, especially in clinical
psychology, the reverse is true; the practitioner makes
discoveries for the researcher to investigate further.
Rigidly to separate research and application is to handicap
both, since these two aspects of psychology should
contribute to each other. Fifth, humanism opposes the
idea that psychologists must always study groups and
support their conclusions with statistics. In contrast, the
humanistic psychologist is often concerned with "the
individual, the exceptional, and the unpredicted, rather
than seeking only to study the regular, the universal, and
the conforming." Finally, the third force psychologist does
not accept what has been called "reductionism": the
view that man can be reduced to "nothing but" a
collection of animal instincts, habits, id-impulses,
reflexes, conditioned responses, or some other basic units.
Man, in the humanist perspective, is an irreducible
individual who is more than the sum of a number of parts.
He is creative, self-directing, and bursting with potential.
He is a whole human being whose behavior can never
totally be determined by environmental or unconscious
influences.

Third force psychology still suffers from the reputation
of being a reactionary movement *against* a lot of things but
not really standing *for* anything. Its reputation is
unfortunate and inaccurate. Although the movement
began as a protest and continues to oppose weaknesses
it sees in experimental and clinical psychology, humanistic
psychology also makes some positive affirmations.

Chief among these is a respect for man's goodness and
capabilities. According to the American Association for

57   Humanistic Psychology,[7] the third force movement has "an ultimate concern with...the dignity and worth of man and an interest in the development of the potential inherent in every person." Instead of reducing human beings to mechanistic reacting organisms (as both behaviorism and psychoanalysis had done) the humanists put "an emphasis on such distinctively human qualities as choice, creativity, valuation, and self-realization."[8] Experimental and clinical psychologists are criticized for placing too much emphasis on human weaknesses, shortcomings, and psychological inadequacies. Although these negative characteristics must be acknowledged, the humanists have stressed that man also has strengths, value, innate goodness, and a great "human potential" for growth.

In addition, third force psychology sees value in the study of subjective experiences. Detached observation is not completely rejected, but accompanied by at least an equal emphasis on participant observation wherein the investigator or therapist empathizes subjectively.[9] It is assumed that empathy can give "personal knowledge" which could never come through the more accepted techniques of experimental or clinical psychology. Because of this emphasis on the subjective, humanists say little about *responses, reactions,* or *habits,* but they have much to say about *values, peak experiences, affection,* and other topics which Skinner might be inclined to dismiss as "fictional fantasies."

A concise description of humanism was given several years ago by Joseph Wood Krutch. He defined the humanist as

> ...anyone who rejects the attempt to describe or account for man wholly on the basis of physics, chemistry, and animal behavior. He is anyone who believes that will, reason, and purpose are real and significant; that value and justice are aspects of a reality called good and evil and rest upon some foundation other than custom; that consciousness is

58

so far from being a mere epiphenomenon that it is the most tremendous of actualities; that the unmeasurable may be significant; or, to sum it all up, that those human realities which sometimes seem to exist only in the human mind are the perceptions, rather than merely the creations, of that mind. He is, in other words, anyone who says that there are more things in heaven and earth than are dreamed of in the positivist philosophy.[10]

As humanistic third force psychology grows in influence, the movement appears to be setting some positive goals for the future. These include:
—development of new, improved, and more diversified scientific methods;
—development of a more positive view of man—one that sees the human personality as dignified, healthy, purposive, creative, and "self-actualizing";
—new emphasis on the study of healthy individuals, in place of the former focus on unhealthy people or on the study of large groups;
—continued attempts to study and understand the whole person, including inner emotions, needs, and potentialities as well as overt behavior; and
—development of a new kind of therapy that de-emphasizes the past, helps people find self-identity and meaning in life, guides individuals into more meaningful relationships with other people, assists persons to develop their potentialities and fulfill their inner needs, and stresses such issues as individual freedom, responsibility, feelings, or values.[11]

Perhaps because of its loosely structured approach to the study of human experience and behavior, third force psychology has attracted and made room for a variety of psychologists and others sympathetic to humanism but best known for highly individualistic theories and therapeutic practices. Described sometimes as the avant garde strain in psychology, these people frequently look to

59   the East or to the occult for their views of reality. Often
their ideas are expressed through articles in *Psychology
Today* magazine. Their interests include such diverse
topics as LSD and psychedelic therapy, witchcraft, gay
liberation, transcendental meditation, dance therapy (it
"helps unleash the bottled-up tensions that make people
feel bad, and, besides that, it's fun"[12]), primal scream
therapy, bio-feedback, sensory deprivation as an approach
to personal growth, dream telepathy, theater-game and
psychodrama groups, gestalt therapy, and a variety of
others. In spite of somewhat unorthodox values and
treatment techniques, these advocates are, for the most
part, serious professionals who practice and believe in
the therapeutic effectiveness of their unique approaches.

As an example of these new approaches to treatment,
we might consider the so-called "body therapies," all of
which involve sensual stimulation, massage, and
manipulation of the physique. The emphasis in these
therapies is less on rationality, disciplined thinking, or
self-control, and more on physical movement or "erotic
awareness of the total body." Exercise, repositioning of
limbs, dancing, structural integration (also known as
Rolfing—a strenuous ten-hour manipulation of the
body), symbolic movements, and such "ancient oriental
body disciplines" as yoga, Tai Chi, Zen awareness
training, chanting, and fasting are all used to stimulate the
senses and create a "free organism."[13]

Much different are the "radical therapies" which claim
to be more political than sensual. In these approaches,
therapy is seen as a life style in which groups are formed
with liberation and revolution as stated goals. Insight
therapies (which emphasize awareness) and encounter
groups (which stress contact) are criticized because they
leave people oppressed. In contrast, the "basic radical
therapy formula" states that liberation = awareness +
contact. According to one of its leading advocates,

> Radical therapy is any one of the following:
> organizing a community to *seize control* of the

way it's run; helping a brother or sister through a
crisis; rooting out our own chauvinism and
mercilessly exposing it in others; focusing on the
social dimensions of oppression and not on
"intrapsychic depression, fear, anger, and so on";
organizing against...war, against polluting
industries, against racist practice; developing a
political/therapy center for young people....[14]

More prominent, perhaps, and certainly less political,
is an approach known as transpersonal psychology.[15]
Like the humanistic third force from which it sprang, this
movement also looks to Masiow as its founder but
sometimes refers to itself as the new "fourth force" in
psychology. Transpersonal psychologists believe that
there is more to man than his body, intelligence,
psychological functioning, or attempts at self-actualization.
It is assumed that man has a spiritual dimension which
includes impulses that move him toward some "ultimate
state." Each individual is free to choose his or her own
"path" toward what is ultimate (trans-personal); the
transpersonal therapist attempts to help counselees
move along in their spiritual pilgrimage. According to one
writer, therapists "help others to have and to
comprehend transcendental, mystical or spiritual
experiences; and they help others to live their daily lives
in ways which foster spiritual fulfillment."[16] Interpretation
and explanation of mystical experiences, meditation,
encouragement, psychic healing techniques, or the use of
astrology and horoscopes are all part of the therapist's
methodology.
    Although transpersonal psychology links itself closely
with the humanistic movement, third force psychologists
have been less than enthusiastic about the birth of this
enfant terrible. Contrasting the two movements, one
writer[17] has argued that there are no such things as
ultimate states, absolutes, or transpersonal experiences.
These are not ideals that are *beyond* man; they are all
human experiences *within* man, at deeper levels of

61   consciousness. Transpersonal psychology, therefore, is criticized for giving assent to an "unconscious desire for perfect security in an ultimate condition of existential oneness or ecstatic communion with some kind, eternally perfect, all loving, absolute spirit. Unfortunately, however, such a desire is only an exercise in self delusion."[18] Stated in less ostentatious language, some humanists apparently fear that the transpersonal psychologists in their ranks are flirting with the idea of a supernatural being or god who is beyond and greater than man.

For a number of reasons, humanistic psychology with its various outgrowths is harder to evaluate than the traditional experimental and clinical approaches. The third force, for example, is extremely diversified and almost impossible to analyze as a unified movement. In addition, the third force has not yet had time to prove itself, making it more difficult for critics to find either weaknesses or strengths. Most of the deficiencies seen in experimental and clinical psychology have been condemned by the humanists, who have a conscious determination to avoid pitfalls of the past. The movement pulsates with an optimistic belief that third force psychology "represents a major breakthrough" capable of improving the science of psychology, even of "changing the course of world history."[19]

Not everyone would agree with such an enthusiastic endorsement, but it may be that the third force currently does represent psychology's greatest hope for the future. The movement acknowledges the faults of contemporary psychological science and is determined to do something about them. The humanists are striving for more flexibility in both their scientific techniques and their perspectives on man. Having criticized the behavioristic and psychoanalytic tendency to view man as little more than a manipulated organism, third force psychology goes on to assert a positive view of human potential and a belief in individual freedom. Humanism challenges long-accepted assumptions that psychology is mainly a study of behavior or of unconscious impulses. It argues that human emotional experiences, values, and hopes are such an important part of man's being that they should be included in any science of mankind.

In reading the humanistic literature, however, I am reminded of the optimism that so often prevails when the voters of a democratic country elect a new government. There is great hope that the lethargy and ineffectiveness of the outgoing regime will be swept away and replaced by new progress and new ways of doing things. The voters and the press rarely criticize the incoming government before it takes office, and even during the first months of the new administration there is willingness to believe the promises and optimistic statements about the good things that are soon to come. But to talk about reform and to bring it to pass are two different things. Governments and politicians are not always able to produce the changes they had promised during the campaign. In a somewhat similar way, the third force, like a new government, has attracted many followers who are dissatisfied with the old psychological regimes and hoping for something better. The new movement is characterized by a lot of optimistic talk about the future. It remains to be seen if this can be followed by the practical progress psychology needs and the humanists so strongly desire. At this early stage of its development, third force psychology is beginning to look like a movement that, while popular, may also be reactionary, overly idealistic, and fragmented.

Several years ago one critic described the new movement as being not a force at all but simply a large group of frustrated individuals "who stand for nothing focal other than a feeling of disaffection from the emphases of recent American psychology."[20] Some humanists are trying to cast off this *reactionary protest image*,[21] which pictures the movement as being opposed to many things but standing for very little that is positive. Nevertheless, the reactionary nature of third force psychology is still obvious in the literature. One gets the impression that

63

some leaders enjoy the image of being "scientific revolutionaries" who protest in ways that parallel revolutionary acts "against other institutions whose rigidly authoritarian positions threatened the course of modern life."[22] In itself, there is nothing wrong with being a revolutionary, scientific or otherwise. Disagreement helps to clarify issues and, by challenging the status quo, mankind throughout history has made significant advances.

Observing the third force movement, however, some outsiders have wondered if a reactionary "feeling of disaffection" with traditional psychology is the only thing that holds the new movement together. The revolutionary image has been strengthened by a secondary movement which has loosely aligned itself with third force psychology. Known by such terms as the "human potential movement," the "encounter-culture," or "experiential psychology," this group included advocates of everything from sensitivity training and encounter groups to nude marathons, spiritualist séances, altered states of consciousness, and a variety of alternative life styles. Some writers have tried to emphasize the secondary and subordinate role that such activities play in the third force movement,[23] but their presence has led at least one influential critic to equate "humanistic psychology" with "human potentialists" and to criticize the former for the excesses of the latter.[24] The third force is seen by some as being not only reactionary but also irresponsible and hardly the panacea that its followers claim.

Such a criticism is of relatively minor importance. Even if its image is tarnished, the third force movement is attracting the sympathetic interest of increasing numbers of psychologists. More significant than the reactionary image, therefore, is the suggestion that the new movement is *overly idealistic* and unrealistic in its optimism.

It is all very well to talk about new methods, new therapy, or a new reunion of psychology with the humanities, but more cautious observers might wonder how the new goals will be implemented or even whether they will work. A behaviorist, Skinner, has accomplished a great deal with his positivist assumptions, rigid experimental methodology, and disbelief in human freedom and dignity. In contrast there is as yet little evidence to show that third force optimism is justified or that the new movement is a viable alternative to more traditional psychology.

Let us consider, as an example, the humanistic belief in man's innate goodness. Third force psychologist Floyd W. Matson has expressed strong opposition both to the old doctrines of original sin or innate depravity and to the new belief in man's aggressiveness. Such a view, he claims, represents a "failure of nerve," "a cop-out," an unwillingness to take responsibility for our actions, a "dehumanizing, depersonalizing and demoralizing force that would move us further down the road to the Brave New World...."[25] As an alternative, it has been proposed that since man is loving, productive, and responsible by nature, all we need do is simply allow our inner potential to realize itself.[26]

At the beginning of this century, liberal theologians held such an optimistic view but two world wars and increasing violence at home led them to modify their beliefs. Sociologists after World War II had great enthusiasm for man's ability to improve his lot, but it soon became clear that the optimistic schemes didn't work as anticipated.[27] Others have put their faith in science, education, or political movements like the Great Society, but none of these has demonstrated that man on his own is getting better and better. Humanist Rollo May is at least willing to acknowledge that within every individual there is evil as well as good.[28] Is there any basis for concluding that the good, rather than the evil, will direct human activities when people are encouraged to disclose themselves, to express their freedom, or to have faith in their abilities? Perhaps the humanists have made the error of thinking that wishing will make it so. Idealistic optimism about man's goodness and innate ability to

65 mold a bright future all by himself is built, at best, on inconclusive evidence.

A further criticism of third force psychology is its *fragmentation*. Apart from dissatisfaction with existing psychology and belief in the innate potential of man, the new movement has no central core or rallying point. Its advocates have a tendency to use vague terms such as "eupsychia," "eigenwelt," "metamotivations," "being," "knowingness," "proactive man," and "existentialism." These lead to communication difficulties within the movement and make it difficult for outsiders to understand what humanistic psychology is all about. In spite of enthusiasm about the movement's future, there is, at least for the present, no clearly defined humanistic theory, no uniquely humanistic therapy, and no agreed-upon research methodology. Further, it is unlikely that these will be forthcoming, since humanists are so strongly motivated to avoid rigidity.

The dilemma of trying to court all methods while marrying none is well illustrated in the following description of third force research techniques:

> Humanistic psychology is in the paradoxical position of having at once a tremendous range of available methods for its work and yet a serious methodological problem. The result is that *there is a very chaotic condition in the whole field* and that a great deal of subjective judgment is involved in trying to sort out that which is truly creative and productive from that which is simply clever or well intentioned. It is not a situation which offers comfort to those who like their lives and their science orderly and their decisions depersonalized....
>
> Humanistic psychology has a tremendous range of available methods. This is so because all the fields of study by which man has, from earliest times, tried to inquire into his own nature and destiny are available: philosophy, religion, history, literature, art, and all other fields make an overwhelming array.

66

> Prayer, meditation, mystical insight, magic,
> contemplation, naturalistic observation,
> introspection, interviews, experiments, surveys—
> all these and more are possible tools to the task.
>   Yet, it is evident, where there is such profusion
> there must be—and indeed *there is—much*
> *confusion, contradiction, and ambiguity....*[29]

Confusion, contradiction, and ambiguity would not
have been tolerated earlier in this century, but we now
seem to have moved into an era when reason, logic, and
rational thought are less important than they were
previously.[30] Since many intellectuals have concluded
that nothing makes sense any more, even the universities
have become centers of mysticism, occultism, altered
states of consciousness, and other nonintellectual
pursuits. It probably would be inaccurate to conclude that
third force psychology is nonintellectual or
anti-intellectual.[31] The movement's sympathy toward and
preference for subjective concepts like personal
experience, inner emotion, felt needs, and existential
values would never have been tolerated by Freud or the
behaviorists. They would have branded it a retreat from the
rational. Possibly the current respect for subjectivity,
impulsiveness, and even intellectual ambiguity may
explain some of the popularity of third force psychology.
According to the new movement, everyone (except
behaviorists, psychoanalysts, and—as we shall
see—some religious believers) is free to "do his own
thing" in psychology and to use his own methods. It is
hardly surprising, therefore, that the third force is both
popular and excessively diversified.

In addition to its reactionary image, apparent idealism,
and excessive fragmentation, a fourth characteristic of
humanistic psychology has been criticized. Critics see it as
a movement with little concern for theory formulation or
research but a great interest in recruiting followers and
arguing for its superiority over traditional approaches to
psychology. The Association for Humanistic Psychology,

according to one book, has produced "some of the most militant rhetoric psychology has witnessed,"[32] rhetoric that is more philosophical, religious, and political than scientific. Such criticism may be unfair, faulting humanistic psychology for not being like the experimental psychology against which it is protesting. Nevertheless it is legitimate to ask if the third force is attempting to replace science and scientific language with philosophy and a humanistic jargon consisting of an "indiscriminate repetitive use of words so full of intricate subtleties that philosophers and linguists have for years struggled with their essence."[33] In itself the latter alternative is not necessarily bad. Human behavior may be so complex that it requires complex descriptive terminology, but if scientific psychology is being replaced by something else, the third force should be honest enough to say so.

In spite of its many commendable features, therefore, third force psychology hardly qualifies as a dramatic "breakthrough that is capable of changing the course of world history" or a major revolution that ranks with the discovery of relativity, the influence of psychoanalysis, or the impact of Christianity.[34] Already the humanists are admitting to confusion, contradiction, and ambiguity, and it is hard for the observer to accept the explanation that this floundering merely reflects the ferment, evolution, and growth of a healthy new field. Freed by their own self-definition from disciplined intellectual precision or scientific rigor, the humanists have built an existential experience-based system which rests on the debatable assumption that total psychic transparency and self-exposure will lead to therapeutic and growth-releasing potential. By de-emphasizing intellectual and reasoning abilities, the humanists have put themselves in danger of reducing man to an experience-directed being who may have freedom but who certainly is without dignity. For the present it would seem that third force psychology, like the experimental and clinical movements from which it arose, has significant weaknesses and limited ability to explain behavior effectively or to promote human welfare.

68   This conclusion, if it is valid, leaves psychology in the uncomfortable position of having little to offer in response to the needs of modern men and women. Students and laypeople who look to psychology for an answer to human problems often come away frustrated and wondering if our science has *anything* of value to contribute. This frustration was dramatically illustrated by a Canadian student whom I met in a little Swiss town near Geneva. He had graduated with a degree in psychology from a large university and had enrolled in graduate school. "But I got discouraged," he said. "Psychology seemed so irrelevant, picayune, and disinterested in human beings." As a result of his frustrations the student decided to look around Europe for a few months while he collected his thoughts. Then he planned to return to graduate school "in sociology, religion, one of the humanities, or some field that is more concerned about man." Certainly this student and others like him could never agree with the happily optimistic statement made by Abraham Maslow back in the 1950s: "I believe that psychologists occupy the most centrally important position in the world today. I say this because all the important problems of mankind... will yield only to a better understanding of human nature, and to this psychology alone applies itself."[35]

Although it may seem paradoxical, I am inclined to agree both with Maslow and with that disillusioned student in Switzerland. Psychology is important and it can be relevant. Thousands of behaviorists, clinicians, humanists, and other psychologists have applied themselves, each in a way that he or she has considered best, to the "better understanding of human nature." We do not completely degrade their efforts if we admit that progress in psychology has been very slow.

In spite of its ills, psychology is not dead and neither does it need to die. There is a bright future for the science of human behavior, but there needs to be a rejuvenation, which, as yet, few people have proposed seriously. There needs to be a reevaluation and reformulation of psychology's most basic presuppositions.

[1]The articles of the American Association for Humanistic Psychology note that "humanistic psychology is primarily an orientation toward the whole of psychology rather than a distinct area or school," but it is interesting to note that Charlotte Buhler, one of the leaders in the new movement, has recently called it a "movement and a school." See Buhler, C., "Basic Theoretical Concepts of Humanistic Psychology," *American Psychologist* **26,** 1971, pp. 378-386.

[2]Rogers was identified as a clinical psychologist in chapter 3, but he has identified himself as being a part of the third force movement and his current interests certainly place him in the humanistic camp. See Rogers, C. R., "Toward a Science of the Person." In Wann, T. W. (ed.), *Behaviorism and Phenomenology,* Chicago: The University of Chicago Press, 1964, pp. 109-133.

[3]Maslow, A. H. *Toward a Psychology of Being.* New York: Harper and Row, 1962.

[4]Two summaries of Maslow's work have recently been published: Goble, Frank, *The Third Force: The Psychology of Abraham Maslow,* New York: Grossman, 1970; and Wilson, Colin, *New Pathways in Psychology: Maslow and the Post-Freudian Revolution,* London: Gollancz, 1972.

[5]The summary of humanistic psychology is based largely on the following sources: Buhler, *op. cit.;* Buhler, Charlotte and Allen, Melanie, *Introduction to Humanistic Psychology,* Monterey, California: Brooks/Cole, 1972; Severin, Frank (ed.), *Humanistic Viewpoints in Psychology,* New York: McGraw-Hill, 1965; and Bugental, James F. T. (ed.), *Challenges of Humanistic Psychology,* New York: McGraw-Hill, 1967.

[6]Bugental, J. F. T. "Humanistic Psychology: A New Breakthrough," *American Psychologist* **18,** 1963, pp. 563-567; and Bugental, J. F. T., "The Challenge That Is Man." In *Challenges of Humanistic Psychology, op. cit.,* pp. 5-11.

[7]Buhler, Charlotte and Bugental, James F. T. *American Association of Humanistic Psychology* (brochure), San Francisco, AAHP, 1965-6.

[8]*Ibid.*

[9]Matson, Floyd W. *Without/Within: Behaviorism and Humanism.* Monterey, California: Brooks/Cole, 1973, p. 19.

[10]Krutch, Joseph Wood. *Human Nature and the Human Condition.* New York: Random House, 1959. Quoted in Severin, *op. cit.,* p. xvii.

[11]For further discussions of humanistic therapy see Buhler and Allen, *op. cit.;* Temerlin, M. K., "On Choice and Responsibility in a Humanistic Psychotherapy," *Journal of Humanistic Psychology* **3,** 1963, 35-48; Kemp, C. S., "Existential Counseling," *The Counseling Psychologist* **2,** 1971, pp. 2-30; Frankl, V., *Man's Search for Meaning: An Introduction to Logotherapy,* New York: Washington Square Press, 1965; and May, Rollo, "Humanism and Psychotherapy," *Pastoral Psychology* **19,** April 1968, pp. 11-17.

[12]Anderson, Walt. "Pas de Psyche," *Human Behavior* **4,** March 1975, pp. 56-60. The quotation is from page 2 of the magazine.

[13]See two articles by S. Keen, "Sing the Body Electric" and "My New Carnality," both in *Psychology Today,* 1970, **4,** pp. 56-61.

[14]Agel, J. (prod.). *The Radical Therapist,* New York: Ballantine, 1971, p. 290.

[15]Much of our discussion of transpersonal psychology is based on two articles by A. J. Sutich: "Transpersonal Psychology: An Emerging Force," *Journal of Humanistic Psychology*, 1968, **8**, pp. 77-79, and "Transpersonal Therapy," *Journal of Transpersonal Psychology*, November 1973, **5**, pp. 1-6.

[16]Weide, T. N. "Varieties of Transpersonal Therapy," *Journal of Transpersonal Psychology*, November 1973, **5**, pp. 7-14.

[17]Chaudhuri, H. "Psychology: Humanistic and Transpersonal," *Journal of Humanistic Psychology*, 1975, **15**, pp. 7-16.

[18]*Ibid.*, p. 12.

[19]Goble, *op. cit.*, p. xii.

[20]Koch, Sigmund, "Psychology and Emerging Conceptions of Knowledge as Unitary." In T. W. Wann, *op. cit.*, p. 44.

[21]See Bugental, James F. T., *Challenges of Humanistic Psychology, op. cit.*, p. viii.

[22]Buhler and Allen, *op. cit.*, p. 76. See also pp. 24, 89.

[23]Matson, *op. cit.*, p. 9.

[24]Koch, Sigmund, "Psychology Cannot Be a Coherent Science," *Psychology Today* **3**, September 1969, pp. 14, 64-8. See especially the last eleven paragraphs of this article.

[25]Matson, *op. cit.*, p. 21.

[26]Brinckerhoff, Robert, "Freudianism, Behaviorism and Humanism." In Matson, *op. cit.*, p. 35.

[27]"The Rediscovery of Human Nature," *Time* **101**, April 2, 1973, pp. 78-81.

[28]*Ibid.*

[29]Bugental, *op. cit.*, p. 79 (italics mine).

[30]The modern rejection of the rational has been discussed by Maddocks, Melvin, "The New Cult of Madness: Thinking As a Bad Habit," *Time*, March 13, 1972, pp. 27, 30; and analyzed by Schaeffer, Francis A., *The God Who Is There*, Chicago: InterVarsity, 1968.

[31]This, however, is the conclusion of Braginsky, B. M. & Braginsky, D. D., *Mainstream Psychology: A Critique*. New York: Holt, Rinehart and Winston, 1974, p. 161.

[32]*Ibid.*, p. 76.

[33]*Ibid.*, p. 81.

[34]Goble, *op. cit.*, p. xii; Bugental, *op. cit.*, p. 345.

[35]Maslow, A. H., "A Philosophy of Psychology: The Need for a Mature Science of Human Nature." In Severin, *op. cit.*, pp. 17-19.

Chapter Five

PSYCHOLOGY

IN THE
RAW

DURING the 1960s when student protests and violence were rocking previously complacent university campuses, some observers noted that the protesters were quick to criticize but much less inclined to offer solutions. "Anybody can find fault," it was sometimes stated, "but it's not so easy to come up with a viable alternative to an existing system, even when that system has a lot of weaknesses."

In many respects the preceding chapters have concentrated on finding fault with psychology as it now exists. Though acknowledging the contributions of experimentalists, clinicians, and humanists, I have freely pointed to their weaknesses and have aligned myself with those who feel that twentieth-century psychology has been weighed in the balances and found wanting.

Most of the published criticisms of psychology have come from North American writers, but recently a British professor named Liam Hudson published an autobiographical account of his education and early teaching experience. His training as a student at Oxford sounds similar to that of budding psychologists in other parts of the world including North America. "We performed experiments," he writes, "that

> ...had about them an air—sometimes arch, sometimes defiant—of contrivance and triviality....we sorted cards, watched flashing lights, pressed bars, and once or twice watched white rats wander disconsolately through poorly constructed mazes. We discovered nothing of much interest, either about rats or about ourselves; and it was never hinted that we might. Our highest ambition was to refute a theory; or, failing that, to lend it conditional support. Any idea that we were there to uncover the mysteries of the human mind, to plumb the depths of the psyche, would have been greeted with embarrassment; the kind of embarrassment that hardens into derision, and eventually into contempt. Just as a man on a desert

island was held to illuminate the moral order, so a rat or monkey or student pressing a bar was thought to illuminate the brain.[1]

Not until much later, after he had earned a Cambridge Ph.D. and begun to do research on the measurement of intelligence and personality, did this professor come to a full realization that his discipline was in failing health. "It has failed to produce a coherent body of scientific law," he complained sadly. "There is little that we have produced in the last fifty years that is, in any sense of that complex word, 'relevant.' "[2]

Professor Hudson has not been content simply to criticize psychology and bemoan its current state of ill health. He, and others like him, have proposed a number of practical ideas (and some not so practical) for reviving and renovating the field. Previously we mentioned the analysis of George Albee, who proposed that psychology could maintain the status quo in hopes that things will get better, develop separate professional schools of psychology with more relevant training programs, merge with existing fields of study like education and social work, or permanently divide into two separate and independent disciplines: professional psychology and scientific psychology.[3] Less drastic but less specific have been the suggestions that psychologists should in some way reevaluate their priorities and goals, deliberately strive to make their science more relevant in solving social problems, do research that stresses persons rather than methods, or focus attention on "the whole man" instead of on the study of isolated elements of behavior.

Many of these solutions have been proposed more than once and some have been tried, but they suffer from one common weakness: they deal with the symptoms of psychology's dilemma rather than with the root cause. It is the thesis of this book that the real source of the current turmoil in psychology is that we have built our science on a foundation of shaky and untenable assumptions. To complain sadly about the current state of psychology or to suggest changes in such things as our methodology and training techniques is to deal only with symptoms. Instead, we must uncover, examine, alter, and be willing if necessary to replace completely the foundational presuppositions on which the science of psychology has thus far been built.

For many years scientists, including psychologists, clung to the belief that their research efforts could be completely neutral and objective. It was rarely acknowledged that psychologists might have presuppositions, philosophical biases, prejudices, superstitions, or values—at least of the kind that would influence their work. Freud, of course, had acknowledged that the scientist's own unconscious conflicts could bias his observation of data or interfere with his therapeutic effectiveness. As a part of his training, therefore, every psychoanalyst was required to be analyzed himself, in the hope that this treatment would make it possible for him as a doctor to be completely neutral and free from value judgments in his work.[4] The behaviorists also recognized the importance of neutrality and lack of bias, but they apparently took it for granted that with sufficient care in one's scientific work it would be possible to accumulate facts in an objective, verifiable, reproducible, and unbiased way.[5] It is not difficult to understand the desire for objectivity and neutrality. The psychologist's desire to be scientific seemed to require that one reject or at least keep control of one's subjective opinions and biases.

To avoid bias in science is a worthy goal, but as we have indicated in earlier chapters, it may also be an unattainable goal. In psychology, instead of dealing with inanimate forces or objects, we study conscious, thinking individuals who can interact with the researcher, help him in his work, or sometimes even hinder him.[6] Even if data collection could be objective, the psychologist's own values, prejudices, beliefs, and presuppositions would probably influence such significant issues as what he studies, how he carries out his research, how he interprets the data, the honesty or dishonesty with which he reports his conclusions, what he chooses to teach his students, and the ways in which he attempts to help distressed people who come for counseling.

Thus, in spite of commendable efforts to control biases, values, and personal assumptions, the psychologist's work, like that of every other scientist, is influenced by an underlying set of presuppositions about man, his world, and his ways of acquiring knowledge. Very often these presuppositions are either accepted with little thought or are completely overlooked,[7] but it is on these foundational assumptions that psychologists have built their science, their profession, and their careers. When problems have arisen, psychologists have tried to refine methodology or subject matter in some way. Rarely have we challenged or even considered the assumptions that determine the methods we choose in the first place and which thus ultimately lead to the data we discover. Seldom do we entertain the possibility that modern psychology might be the visible superstructure of a science built on a largely unexamined but tenuous presuppositional foundation. If we want a solid, relevant, and healthy discipline, we must begin not by shoring up the tottering skyscraper, but by reevaluating and rebuilding the foundation.

At this point it might be tempting to criticize those who, consciously or otherwise, just accepted the presuppositions on which psychology was being built. But most of the early pioneers, like many psychologists today, probably never thought much about their philosophical assumptions. If they had, they still might have chosen the presuppositions on which psychology currently rests. It is only now, almost 100 years after psychology's beginning as a separate discipline, that we begin to see how some of our foundations might be inadequate and in need of revision.

Before we can bring about change, however, we must

identify the assumptions already existing, show how these affect the psychologist's work, and attempt to assess their merits. This is a difficult task, because any list of assumptions proposed will surely be challenged. In 1958, Meehl suggested that only three philosophical presuppositions—determinism, materialist monism, and intersubjective confirmability—could be accepted by all psychologists as rock-bottom ideas on which to build their science.[8] But even these three issues are viewed differently by individual psychologists. Hammes, for example, has shown that determinism can be defined in at least ten different ways and that some of these varieties of determinism are incompatible with others.[9] In the remainder of this chapter, I would like to suggest that when psychology is stripped to the raw, to its barest essentials, the discipline rests on at least five presuppositions. Most of these are philosophical although some might be considered methodological. The basis on which their science is built can be summarized for most psychologists in a few words: "I acknowledge the importance of *empiricism, determinism, relativism, reductionism, and naturalism.*"

Empiricism is perhaps the most widely accepted and firmly held of all the presuppositions underlying psychology. In the words of one writer, "psychology's most general characteristics today are a nearly universal faith in empiricism and a heavy dependence upon experimental methods as means of acquiring greater understanding of human behavior."[10] The early psychologists concluded that physics and other established natural sciences were characterized by the objective examination of observable facts, most of which were discovered by scientific experiments. In its haste to become established as a science, psychology tried to copy this approach. Nobody ever said much about *truth*—a philosophical and theological term which psychologists have preferred to avoid—but an implicit assumption underlying psychological research was that

78   the only things we can believe and accept as true are the
observations we experience with our own senses. Perhaps
there is no better statement of this than that of a
psychologist who declared that he had "no doubt
whatever" that in comparison with other techniques
"the methods of empirical psychology are socially more
hygienic, or to use an older and more robust phrase,
morally better."[11]

Belief in the superiority of empiricism has expressed
itself in different ways. Experimentalists would agree that
empirical psychology involves the use of "controlled
experiment and observation rather than the intuitive
exercise of imagination."[12] The experimentalist tends to
prefer a large number of subjects, precise measuring
devices, statistical analyses of data, and controlled
observation techniques that can be clearly described
and replicated by others. In contrast, Freud and many other
clinicians who also profess a belief in empiricism have
sought to make accurate observation of individual
patients and then to validate the accuracy of these
observations by observing other patients. Freud's
data-collecting methods have been severely criticized,[13]
but undoubtedly he considered them to be reliable and
valid empirical procedures. Humanists also seek to
make accurate observations about man, and thus they too
could be called empiricists, although third force
psychology (unlike the other two approaches) is willing to
include observation of inner feelings and experiences as
a valid part of research.[14] Empiricism is viewed in so many
different ways that perhaps we should use modifying
adjectives to indicate what we mean by the term.
Experimental empiricism, for example, could be
distinguished from clinical empiricism or from the
experiential empiricism of third force psychology. Even
though empiricism is viewed differently, almost all
psychologists agree that empirical observation (however
they define it) is basic to their science and of more value in
studying man than, say, rational deduction or revelation
from some divine authority.

79   Empiricism assumes that accurate observation is
possible—a debatable conclusion even in the natural
sciences. Introductory psychology textbooks sometimes
describe an event that took place over 200 years ago at
the Greenwich Observatory in England. The Astronomer
Royal dismissed his assistant for inaccuracy because the
poor young fellow didn't see the sun hit the mid-line of
the telescope until a split second after it had been seen by
his superior. This controversial firing stimulated some
people to design experiments that demonstrated individual
differences in the ways that scientists see their data. Even
the same individual, it has since been concluded, might
see things a little differently every time he looks. There
are ways to control for this bias,[15] of course, but even with
controls we can never be sure that our observations are
completely free of misperception. In the last analysis, all
empirical knowledge rests on the personal subjective
experience of the researcher.[16] None of us can be a
detached and neutral observer, who approaches the
subject matter with a completely open mind. We come
with expectations and attitudes which distort our
perceptions and lead us to observe some things while we
unintentionally overlook others.

Even if we could make unbiased empirical
observations, however, there is still the problem of the
scientist's influence on the data. This is especially true in
psychology, where the observer's activities and wishes
have a subtle effect on how the experimental subject
reacts. Most of the human subjects in psychological
experiments are college students, and many of these are
volunteers.[17] Such people are frequently impressed with
the fact that their behavior as subjects will be contributing
data to "scientific research." The volunteers want to be
cooperative and frequently they behave in ways they think
will please the observer, even though they know they
would react differently if they weren't being watched.[18]
Apparently, therefore, the psychologist's expectations
influence not only his interpretation of the data, but also
the data themselves. This is true even when the subjects

80

are white rats.[19] The very act of making an empirical observation changes the data and makes them in some respects biased and abnormal.

Until recently a belief in the superiority of the empirical approach was so widely accepted that psychological literature rarely entertained the possibility that there might be other efficient ways to learn about man. Empiricism is still a firmly grounded assumption of psychology but, if the humanistic literature is any indication,[20] at least some psychologists are coming to realize that there may be more to the universe than can be seen through scientific methods. To assume that there is no truth other than empirically derived truth is to make a nonempirical leap of faith and to put forth a conclusion for which there is no evidence whatsoever, scientific or otherwise.

Determinism is another rock-bottom assumption on which psychology rests. The view that behavior is determined by some prior cause or causes gives the psychologist his reason for existing. If we can assume that behavior is caused, our purpose becomes that of discovering the causes so that eventually we can understand, predict, and control what people do. In a recent study of 200 faculty members at the University of Michigan it was found that psychologists more than any other group of faculty members expressed belief in determinism and in the view that freedom is a figment of the imagination.[21]

Although most psychologists could be classified as determinists, not all believe that behavior is completely determined. Skinner and many behaviorists maintain that human actions are entirely determined and that individual freedom is an illusion.[22] Freud and his followers, while admitting that humans might have a little freedom, nevertheless concluded that most behavior is molded by unconscious forces over which the individual has little if any control. At the opposite extreme, third force psychologists tend to believe that human actions result from human free will. Men and women, it is argued,

81   determine their own actions. They are largely the masters of their fate rather than victims of forces that control them against their will.

According to Paul Meehl, the deterministic assumption may take three forms. First, there is *methodological determinism* which is little more than a working assumption that guides our activities as psychologists.

> Human behavior seems to exhibit regularities (laws), to be susceptible of rational causal explanations (theories), and to be largely controllable by the use of these laws and theories; let us therefore...operate provisionally on the working assumption that any behavior domain (whether it be learning fractions, drinking beer, being psychoanalyzed, composing symphonies, falling in love, translating Aramaic, or whatever) is orderly, predictable, 'lawful' (in the scientific sense).... If these laws hold strictly, well and good; if they are at best probabilistic, we will settle for that, since they will still be very useful.[23]

Meehl believes that all or nearly all psychologists would accept such a general working hypothesis. Such a view of mankind says that at least some behavior may be determined, lawful, predictable, and able to be studied scientifically.

Empirical determinism assumes that since we have had some success in discovering laws it seems likely that all behavior does, "in fact, follow exceptionless regularities. Apparent exceptions are very probably due to incomplete information and, pending further investigation, will be assumed as such."[24] This view is still popular but perhaps is being held by fewer and fewer psychologists, especially those in the third force movement.

Metaphysical determinism holds that all psychological events reflect natural laws and that all behavior is determined in accordance with these laws.

82

Such rigid adherence to determinism raises some difficulties for psychology. As we have seen, psychological determinism may contradict the widely accepted Heisenberg theory of physics which states that submicroscopic events do not occur in an orderly, cause-effect relationship. Further, metaphysical determinism eliminates personal responsibility and individual choice, since the person whose behavior is determined cannot be free to mold his or her own behavior. This kind of determinism also robs humanity of freedom and dignity, as Skinner has so clearly shown. Perhaps hardest of all to accept, it forces each of us to conclude that we cannot act voluntarily since our thoughts and actions all result from prior causes beyond our immediate control.

If we were to draw a line similar to the following, all psychologists would be somewhere between the two extremes.

All behavior without exception is determined.	*Human behavior is completely free of determining influences.*

Skinner would be close to or at the left end of the scale; humanists would tend to be toward the opposite end; others might be in the middle. The relative merits of different positions on the scale are debatable, but using empirical psychological methods, it is impossible to prove which position is closest to being correct. The rational method of philosophy might be able to shed some light on the issue,[25] but few psychologists are interested in reading philosophy. It's more likely that most of us simply place ourselves on the determinism-freedom scale at a point that best fits our personal values, prejudices, and beliefs.

Another presupposition influencing the psychologist's work is *relativism*. This is the assumption that there are

83

no absolute standards of right or wrong, no absolute truths, and no absolute beliefs. According to relativism, all decisions, ethical choices, and interpretations of data vary in accordance with the observer's social situation and personal point of view.

Relativism has been lauded in psychology as a necessary alternative to rigid authoritarian views about man and morality which were widely held in the previous century.[26] Relativism, it is argued, frees individuals to make their own choices, choose their own values, develop their own life philosophies, find their own meaning to the world, and pursue their own methods of discovering truth.[27]

If we have no absolutes, however, how does one make a decision about what is true, accurate, or morally right? For many the answer is found in pragmatism, a view that grew out of the writings of William James and has since been called "the dominant philosophy in contemporary American culture." Pragmatism emphasizes the practical and concludes that truth is simply what works. If something is workable, the pragmatist says, it must be right; if it doesn't work, it is wrong. According to such a view, truth is relative and subject to change: just because something worked last week, yesterday, or even ten minutes ago is no guarantee that it will function again. In a rapidly changing society, pragmatism is seen by many as our only guide to truth. This is clearly illustrated by Hall and Lindzey in a well-known textbook on personality theory. Theories, they maintain, can never be evaluated as true or false. The best theory is the one that at present works better than all others.[28]

If one accepts the thesis that there can be no absolute certainty about anything, then the best the scientist can do is to determine how probable it is that an event will occur, that a conclusion is valid, or that one thing will cause another. In the final analysis, all scientific data are seen as probable data, based on changing circumstances and best expressed in statistical terms. In experimental psychology, for example, we agree to accept a

84

conclusion only when it reaches the .05 or some other level of probability.

Regretfully, relativism (with its accompanying acceptance of pragmatism and probability) leaves psychology "up in the air" with no unifying force that can tie it together. Psychological "truth" must be seen as something that changes from day to day, and it is evident that there can be as many interpretations of the data as there are psychologists. The assumption of relativism means that psychology must be content with the conclusion that we will never know anything for sure, that any absolute certainty about human nature is forever unattainable.[29] We can't even be sure about our conclusion that "there are no absolutes and everything is relative." This declaration is in itself an absolute statement, but it is inconsistent to state with absolute certainty that all things are relative. In order not to contradict himself the relativist would have to add that "there are no absolute truths except this one."

Thus relativism leaves the psychologist with no firm basis for knowing what is true about man. It also leaves him with no solid ethical foundation to guide his counseling, his scientific activities, or his personal life. In formulating its widely acclaimed code of ethics, the American Psychological Association proceeded empirically by pooling the carefully considered judgments of a number of responsible psychologists[30] and concluded that the basis of right and wrong should be what the majority thinks. But the majority could be wrong and a code of ethics based on popular opinion is a standard that the relativist can choose to ignore if he has a different personal perspective on what is right or wrong.

By assuming that absolute truth is nonexistent and thus unattainable, relativism leaves each person free to make his own decisions about what is just or unjust, good or bad. Some would argue that this is a desirable position, but it is also an unstable position in which all truths and moral judgments can shift with the changing opinions, fads, and events of the times.

85   A fourth issue influencing the psychologist's work is *reductionism*. This is the assumption that all behavior, human and otherwise, can be reduced to or divided into smaller units that are easier to investigate scientifically. Many psychologists have maintained that the best way to study man is to reduce his actions to conditioned responses, synapses, hormone actions, self-concepts, id impulses, or some other basic units which can be carefully measured and analyzed. Science is seen as a process of uncovering minute facts one at a time and hoping that eventually we will have enough little nuggets of data to build a firm and well-established body of truth. One of my professors used a picturesque analogy when he proposed that science is like chipping at a huge rock. We chip off a tiny piece here and there, and by analyzing the pieces, eventually we are able to understand the composition of the entire boulder.

But what happens next? We can break the boulder into powder but then we no longer have a rock. Similarly, human behavior might be divided *ad infinitum* into little pieces that can be measured and analyzed rigorously, but what we are studying then is no longer human behavior; it is physiology or biology or something else. Reductionism makes the questionable assumption that analysis of parts leads to increased understanding of the whole, that complicated problems can be solved by investigating issues that are simpler or more obvious, and that the whole of man's behavior is nothing more than the sum of its parts.

Closely related to this viewpoint is what one writer has called "nothing-buttery" and another has termed "nothing-buttism."[31] This is the view that human behavior and other phenomena can be seen as *nothing but* something simpler. Man is sometimes described as being nothing but an animal; memory is nothing but a reaction of some sort in the brain. Nothing-buttery is apparent with special force when psychologists attempt to explain religion. Belief in God, for example, may be viewed as nothing but superstition; conversion experiences are nothing but individual reactions to the manipulative techniques of some evangelist or religious zealot; faith healing is nothing but the removal of hysterical symptoms. Very often, of course, these explanations may be correct. However, "nothing but" thinking leads to the erroneous conclusion that by reducing a phenomenon to its underlying components, we can explain it and even explain it away. Attempts, therefore, are made to explain away love, hope, expectation, excitement, anger, or sin by finding the psychological or physiological foundation underlying the behavior.[32]

Such reductionism was challenged by gestalt psychologists many years ago. More recently, the third force movement has insisted that man is too complex to be reduced to habits, test scores, physiological drives, or other mechanistic and reductionistic terms.[33] Once again, therefore, we appear to have a continuum with strict reductionists like Skinner at one end, humanists who oppose reductionism at the other end, and the rest of us somewhere in between. There is no disagreement over whether psychological processes should be explained in the simplest terms possible; almost all psychologists would profess a belief in the "law of parsimony." The issue, rather, is how much—if at all—man can be reduced to smaller units of analysis and still maintain his uniqueness as a human being. This issue cannot be decided empirically. To a large extent what we conclude about reductionism is a matter of personal opinion. It is an assumption influencing how we approach the study of man, what we look for in our research, and what we accept as scientific data. The reductionist, because of his views, will continue to use his unique measuring techniques to study minute aspects of human behavior. The critic of reductionism will use different techniques and attempt to study man in his wholeness.

Before leaving the issue of reductionism we might consider briefly the mechanistic viewpoint which assumes that man is only a complex machine. This view

87

has been stated in an extreme form by an engineer who once described man as

> ...a complete, self-contained, totally-enclosed power plant, available in a variety of sizes, and reproducible in quantity. He is relatively long-lived, has made major strides toward solving the spare-parts problem. He is water-proof, amphibious, operates on a wide variety of fuels, enjoys thermostatically-controlled temperature, circulating fluid-heat, evaporative cooling, has sealed, lubricated bearings, audio and optical direction and range finders, sound and sight recording, audio and visual communication, and is equipped with an automatic control called a brain.

The view that man is really a type of machine, first suggested by Greek philosophy, has received new emphasis with the widespread development of computers. Some psychologists, especially those who accept determinism and reductionism, have now come to think of man as a giant computer who receives input stimulations from his environment, processes this information, stores some of it in his memory "system," and then produces "output" in the form of responses.

The problem with this view is that it depersonalizes man and sometimes causes people to feel that they are being treated like robots rather than human beings. The psychologist is likely to reply that the mechanistic view of man is simply a model, a way of looking at people which nobody takes to be an accurate picture of reality.[34] But it is a short and easy step to move from thinking that man is *like* a machine to thinking that he *is* a machine; from describing the brain as analogous to a computer to concluding that the brain *is* a complex computer. It is then, to use Buber's terms,[35] that the psychologist begins to treat others as an "it" to be manipulated and dissected rather than as a "thou" to be respected and understood.

88   Last in our list of presuppositions that influence psychologists is the position of *naturalism*. This is the view that there is no God, that man alone is sovereign in the earth and possibly in the universe, that human destiny lies in our own hands, and that all behavior without exception results from the operation of natural forces which scientists seek to understand and perhaps control. Erich Fromm has stated this view concisely. Man, he wrote, "must accept responsibility for himself. There is no meaning to life except the meaning man gives his life by the unfolding of his powers...(Man is alone) in a universe indifferent to his fate...there is no power transcending him which can solve his problems for him."[36] The naturalist concludes that man is on his own in a world that, by chance, has come to be organized and completely orderly.

Naturalism is firmly held among most psychologists. Anything supernatural is viewed with skepticism, sometimes with derision. In spite of an increasing popular interest in the supernatural, psychologists (with a few notable exceptions) have avoided serious consideration of the subject. Someone has suggested that people once talked freely about religion but were embarrassed to discuss sex; now the situation is reversed.

Several years ago, Paul Tournier observed that

> in order to evolve, science had to adopt a certain point of view and to refuse to depart from it. This involved the conventional *a priori* assumption of the exclusion of transcendence. Science had to set transcendence aside because all scientific curiosity disappears as soon as the cause of any phenomenon is attributed to God. In order to proceed scientifically, psychology must do the same....

But Tournier then makes an unusual suggestion.

> In setting aside transcendence it (psychology) ought not...to deny it. Scientific psychology moves

89

within a frame of reference which limits its outlook strictly to the point of view it has adopted. But on a higher scale there is a synthesized psychology which steps outside this convention, and puts together the two pictures seen respectively by scientific and by spiritual psychology, each observing from its own individual viewpoint.[37]

A psychologist, who, like Fromm, believes solely in naturalism is likely to approach his work differently than an individual who, like Tournier, believes that supernatural forces can affect behavior. A naturalist, for example, might study personality, individual differences, perception (or even ESP), and altered states of consciousness with no thought that God or some other nonhuman being could influence these psychological processes. A supernaturalist would at least acknowledge the possibility of nonhuman influences and might even seek to discover how these forces operate, how they determine the individual's values and outlook in life, or how they could be used as a healing force in counseling.

We psychologists are a diversified group of people who differ from one another in our interests, values, skills, innate ability, and choice of work. We also differ in the philosophical assumptions that influence the way we view the world and approach our vocational tasks. Some are more optimistic, idealistic, behavioristically inclined, or existentially oriented than others. All of us have some recognized or unrecognized views about empiricism, determinism, relativism, reductionism, and naturalism. Such philosophical assumptions are pretty much accepted as valid without our giving them a lot of thought. Psychological journals rarely discuss presuppositions[38] and neither, evidently, do psychology professors. But foundational beliefs are extremely important. They dictate how we approach the study of man and they shape the picture of how man emerges and is accepted. Without a frame of reference built on basic assumptions it would be impossible to observe anything with precision, and psychology could never hope to advance as a science or academic discipline.

We must realize, however, that guiding assumptions can limit our outlook and constrict our thinking. Skinner, for example, has been severely criticized because he has assumed that his empirical method is the only valid approach for psychology. This assumption has led him to conclude that anything his method cannot detect must be nonexistent.[39]

Psychologists need to ask whether the more commonly accepted presuppositions in our science have limited us too much. Have they contributed to our overemphasis on method, to our fascination with minute facts, to our de-emphasis on relevant human issues, to our seeming inability to solve human problems, and to our failure to offer meaning and hope in an age of despair? To become aware of our presuppositions is an important first step toward rebuilding psychology, but as we have suggested earlier, it is not enough. In addition, each of us must be willing to evaluate, alter, or even eliminate some of our current assumptions. If better and more fruitful assumptions can be found, we must be willing to replace some of our old foundations—even if that new core of psychology gets us into the area of religion.

Footnotes
Chapter 5

[1]Hudson, Liam. *The Cult of the Fact*. London: Jonathan Cape, 1972, p. 40.

[2]*Ibid.*, p. 111.

[3]Albee, George W. "The Uncertain Future of Clinical Psychology," *American Psychologist* **25**, 1970, pp. 1071-1080.

[4]Kubie, L. S. *Practical and Theoretical Aspects of Psychoanalysis*. New York: International Universities Press, 1950.

[5]Watson, J. B. *Psychology From the Standpoint of a Behaviorist* (2nd ed.). New York: Lippincott, 1924, p. 1.

[6]Orne, Martin T. "On the Social Psychology of the Psychological Experiment: With Particular Reference to Demand Characteristics and their Implications," *American Psychologist* **17**, pp. 776-783.

[7]At a meeting of eight or ten Ph.D. psychologists who met together to discuss an earlier draft of this book manuscript, none could remember ever having discussed presuppositions during their time in graduate school. The need for a study of psychology's assumptions

91

has been stressed by several writers, including Hudson, *op. cit.*, and Giorgi, Amedeo, *Psychology as a Human Science,* New York: Harper & Row, 1970.

[8]Meehl, Paul, *et al. What, Then, Is Man?* St. Louis: Concordia, 1958, pp. 78-86.

[9]Hammes, John A. *Humanistic Psychology: A Christian Interpretation.* New York: Grune & Stratton, 1971.

[10]Walker, Edward L. *Psychology as a Natural and Social Science.* Belmont, California: Brooks/Cole, 1970, p. 2.

[11]Broadbent, D. E. "In Defense of Empirical Psychology," *Bulletin of the British Psychological Society* **23,** 1970, p. 95 (italics mine).

[12]Shotter, John and Gauld, Alan. "The Defense of Empirical Psychology," *American Psychologist* **26,** 1971, pp. 460-466.

[13]Hall, C. S. and Lindzey, G. *Theories of Personality* (2nd ed.). New York: Wiley, 1970.

[14]Bugental, James F. T. (ed.). *Challenges of Humanistic Psychology.* New York: McGraw-Hill, 1967. See part three: "Research Areas and Methods."

[15]See, for example, Simon, Julian L., *Basic Research Methods in Social Science: The Art of Empirical Investigation.* New York: Random House, 1969, chapters 6, 7, 8.

[16]Rogers, C. R. "Some Thoughts Regarding the Current Philosophy of the Behavioral Sciences," *Journal of Humanistic Psychology* **5,** 1965, pp. 182-194.

[17]Smart, R. "Subject Selection Bias in Psychological Research," *Canadian Psychologist* **7,** 1966, pp. 115-121.

[18]Orne, M. T. "On the Social Psychology of the Psychological Experiment: With Particular Reference to Demand Characteristics and Their Implications," *American Psychologist;* Rosenthal, R. *Experimenter Effects in Behavioral Research.* New York: Appleton-Century-Crofts, 1966; Brandt, Lewis W., "Science, Fallacies, and Ethics," *Canadian Psychologist* **12,** 1971, pp. 231-242.

[19]Hudson, *op. cit.,* p. 168.

[20]See, for example, Royce, Joseph R., "Metaphoric Knowledge and Humanistic Psychology." In Bugental, *op. cit.,* pp. 20-28.

[21]Walker, *op. cit.,* chapter 3.

[22]Skinner, B. F. *Beyond Freedom and Dignity.* New York: Alfred A. Knopf, 1971.

[23]Meehl, Paul, *et al. What, Then Is Man?* St. Louis: Concordia, 1958, pp. 79-81.

[24]*Ibid.,* p. 81.

[25]Hammes, *op. cit.*

[26]Kagan, Jerome. "On the Need for Relativism," *American Psychologist* **22,** 1967, pp. 131-142.

[27]Peterson, James A. *Counseling and Values: A Philosophical Examination.* Scranton, Pennsylvania: International Textbook Company, 1970.

[28]Hall and Lindzey, *op. cit.,* p. 598.

[29]Hammes, *op. cit.*

[30]American Psychological Association. "Ethical Standards of Psychologists." *American Psychologist* **18,** 1963, pp. 56-60.

[31]Donald M. MacKay first suggested the term "nothing-buttery." See

92

MacKay, D. M., *The Clockwork Image,* Downers Grove, Illinois: InterVarsity, 1974, p. 43. The term "nothing-buttism" is in Farnsworth, K. E., "Embodied Integration," *Journal of Psychology and Theology* **2,** 1974, pp. 116-124.

[32] MacKay, *ibid.*

[33] Bugental, James F. T. "Humanistic Psychology: A New Breakthrough," *American Psychologist* **18,** 1963, pp. 563-567. According to the Association of Humanistic Psychology brochure, the third force emphasizes "such distinctly human qualities as choice, creativity, valuation, and self-realization, as opposed to thinking about human beings in mechanistic and reductionist terms."

[34] In another context I have argued this way myself. See Collins, Gary R., "Three Perspectives on Men and Machines—I," *Journal of the American Scientific Affiliation,* 1970, pp. 135-6.

[35] Buber, M. *I and Thou.* New York: Scribner, 1958.

[36] Fromm, E. *Man for Himself.* New York: Rinehart, 1947, p. 445.

[37] Tournier, Paul. *The Person Reborn.* New York: Harper & Row, 1966, pp. 24-5.

[38] For an interesting exception see Amundson, Norman E. and Willson, Stanley, "The Effect of Different Reality Perspectives on Psychotherapy," *Journal of Psychology and Theology,* **1,** Vol. 3, 1973, pp. 22-27.

[39] Hammes, John A. "Beyond Freedom and Dignity: Behavioral Fixed Delusion?" *Journal of Psychology and Theology,* **1,** Vol. 3, 1973, pp. 8-14.

Chapter Six

PSYCHOLOGY

IN CONFLICT WITH RELIGION

95   DURING the course of its history, psychology has never
           shown much interest in religion. General psychology
           books tend to give the topic scant if any attention. Apart
           from a few classic studies like those of James, Freud, and
           Allport,[1] the topic of religious behavior has been largely
           bypassed by psychological writers. As it struggled to
           become an accepted science, psychology had to untangle
           itself from the philosophical-religious traditions of the
           past, and relatively few psychologists have wanted to give
           even a hint of interest in theological issues. The natural
           sciences, which served as a model for psychology, long
           ago challenged traditional views of God and creation,
           replacing them with a confident belief that deities and
           supernatural forces were no longer needed to explain
           how the physical world works. It is not surprising that
           many psychologists reached the same conclusion.
           Philosopher Bertrand Russell contended that religion is
           based both on a fear of the unknown and on an irrational
           hope that some kind of "elder brother in the sky" exists
           to solve all of our problems. Russell confidently predicted
           that as science advanced, religion would retreat and be
           of no further importance.[2] Thus, natural scientists focused
           their attention on issues other than religion, and
           psychologists did likewise.
              Although science has tried to abandon religion and
           traditional theological tenets, it has not been able to
           eliminate beliefs, values, and philosophical assumptions.
           Faith in God has been replaced by faith in human
           potential. The authority of the Bible or church has given
           way to a belief in the trustworthiness of empirical data
           alone. A belief in theological and moral absolutes has
           been replaced by a faith in relativism and situational
           ethics. Psychologists, like other scientists, have discovered
           that although they differ from one another in their
           individual assumptions and attitudes about the world,
           each person believes in something. Often these beliefs
           and presuppositions are accepted uncritically and
           sometimes without awareness of their existence. But as
           we have tried to show in earlier chapters, our underlying,

sometimes unrecognized, assumptions determine how we approach our work and how we handle our data. It is not wrong to criticize or reject traditional religious presuppositions in hopes of finding something better, but it would be unreasonable to conclude *a priori* that all systems of belief are bad or unimportant. Every individual and every science has an underlying belief system that might also be termed a religion. Some of these beliefs are theistic; others are not.

It is the theistic beliefs, those dealing with God and the supernatural, that psychologists have been most inclined to criticize. Some critics have attacked the underlying premises of theistic religion. More often, psychologists have argued that religious beliefs are of no importance to the study of human behavior, and in some cases that theistic religion might be harmful.

Experimental psychologists, including those in the behaviorist tradition, tend to treat religion in one or more of three ways: they ignore it, they dismiss it as being irrelevant, or they explain it away. J. B. Watson, who was among those who ignored religion, evidently worked on the assumption that intelligent people could have neither time for nor interest in something as unscientific as religion. Concepts like "soul," "spirit," or "mind" were deliberately thrown out of the behaviorist vocabulary and sphere of interest. Since a concept like "God" could not be seen with behaviorist techniques, and since God's behavior was not observable, it was assumed that deities and spiritual things did not exist. Today many behaviorists might agree that the existence of God is a possibility, but since he cannot be observed scientifically, tested psychologically, defined operationally, or measured precisely, he is of no interest to scientific investigators. To be noticed by behaviorists or acknowledged as a possible influence on human behavior, a deity would have to reveal himself in a way that could be detected by experimental techniques.

To some experimentalists, religion is simply

97   irrelevant. For researchers who work with animals or study physiological reactions, it must seem that religion has no bearing at all on their work. Anything religious is dismissed by such experimentalists as serving no useful function, doing nothing to increase our understanding of human behavior, making no contribution to the advancement of scientific psychology, and probably doing little if anything to help meet human needs. Like many other scientists, these researchers refuse to become involved with anything that cannot be studied scientifically. Religion is assumed to be unimportant because it is nonscientific and of no relevance to the scientist's work.

A third approach of behaviorists is to explain away religious behavior. With amused tolerance, Skinner has described the behavior of his grandmother who once showed him the coals in the kitchen stove and pointed out that this was what hell would be like.[3] Later in his life Skinner concluded that such beliefs and religious behavior could be adequately explained by the principles of reinforcement. A religious leader molds the thinking and behavior of his followers by demonstrating that desired behavior is reinforced, at least partially, and that "sin" is not reinforced but even punished. One may talk about things like heaven, hell, temptation, sin, and virtue, but, in spite of this unique religious language, the techniques of behavior control used in a catechism class differ in no way from techniques widely utilized by educators, governments, or economists.[4] A believer in religion might protest that God works even in those events which could be explained according to natural means. Skinner and the vast majority of behaviorists would reply that religious explanations are no longer necessary when you can account for something by simpler and more easily defined scientific concepts.

Although he was neither an experimentalist nor a behaviorist, William James worked in the empirical tradition when he set himself the "laborous" task of attempting "to extract from the privacies of religious

98

experience some general facts which can be defined in formulas upon which everybody may agree."[5] James limited his research to the analysis of religious writings and biographies; later investigators attempted to utilize quantitative and experimental techniques.[6] These studies have contributed somewhat to our understanding of religious experience, but as Thouless has suggested, a mere accumulation of quantitative answers to specific questions about religion may lead to an imperfect and at best limited understanding of religion as a whole.[7] There may be more to religion and religious experience than can be explained within the confines of behaviorism or experimental psychology in general.

Unlike experimental psychologists who are often able to ignore religion as they go about their research, clinical psychologists must deal with the subject at least when it comes up in counseling. The prevalence of religious ideas in the thinking of neurotic and psychotic people has led many clinical psychologists to see religion as a harmful crutch which prevents people from facing problems in a realistic and satisfying way. Albert Ellis, for example, in his no-nonsense "rational-emotive" approach to therapy, is highly critical of religion. He views it as a hindrance to mental health and has no hesitation in attacking it during the therapeutic interview.[8]

It was Freud, however, who first and most decisively attacked religion from a psychological point of view. Sitting in an office surrounded by statues of Buddha, images of Greek gods, and other religious objects,[9] Freud wrote several papers and books that attempted to analyze why people are religious.[10] An atheist himself who did not believe in the existence of any supernatural being, Freud nevertheless had great interest in religion. He believed that religious people were both immature and neurotic.

In *Totem and Taboo,* for example, Freud concluded that religion had its origin in the Oedipus complex of

99

primeval man.[11] Religion, he proposed, is "nothing other" than the projection of individual hang-ups and immaturities into the other world. "At bottom God is nothing other than an exalted father.... What constitutes the root of every form of religion (is) a longing for the father."[12] It is not surprising, Freud continued, that man should think of God as a greatly exalted father, "for only such a one could understand the needs of the sons of men, or be softened by their prayers and placated by the signs of their remorse."[13] When the authority of the father collapses, people lose their religious faith—which was Freud's explanation for the defection from religion seen so often in young people.[14] The same thing was assumed to occur in whole cultures. As they mature, societies no longer need to depend on a deified father image; thus religion is largely abandoned.

Freud's views on the origins of religion are not widely accepted, but his conclusions about the illusory nature of religion are popular among psychologists. Religious doctrines, he wrote,

> ...are all illusions, they do not admit of proof, and no one can be compelled to consider them as true or to believe in them.... These (religious) ideas protect man in two directions: against the dangers of nature and fate, and against the evils of human society itself.... Countless people find their one consolation in the doctrines of religion, and only with their help can they endure life.... Thus religion (is)...the universal obsessional neurosis of humanity.... The effect of the consolations of religion may be compared to that of a narcotic.... The true believer is in a high degree protected against the danger of certain neurotic afflictions; by accepting the universal neurosis he is spared the task of forming a personal neurosis.[15]

Freud concluded that religion is like a "sleeping draught" or a mass tranquilizer which neurotic people have leaned on over the years in order to maintain their personal stability. Freud fully expected, however, that with the help of science, people would progress to the point where religious tranquilizers would no longer be needed. Religion is like a childhood neurosis, he wrote, "and (we are)...optimistic enough to assume that mankind will overcome this neurotic phase, just as so many children grow out of their similar neuroses."[16]

Jung, Fromm, and a number of other psychiatrists and clinical psychologists challenged Freud's views of religion, but over the years many other clinicians have tended to accept the conclusion that religion is archaic, inhibiting, immature, and often harmful. When such criticisms are offered, they are usually based on two assumptions, both of questionable validity. First, since the proposed realities of religion cannot be observed satisfactorily by science, it is assumed that there are no such realities. Second, it is assumed that we get an accurate picture of religion by studying the beliefs and behavior of people who are emotionally disturbed.[17]

The first assumption is an argument from ignorance rather than from knowledge. It is reminiscent of the confident Soviet cosmonaut who returned from a space trip and announced that God did not exist because he had not been seen in space. The problem here is not with God; it is with the limitations of science and scientific methodology. By definition, science must rely on the senses and on measurement to obtain truth. But the supernatural, if it exists, may not be apprehensible that way. The scientific method is only one means of learning about the world; other means include logical deduction, revelation from an authority, and intuition. Scientific knowledge in itself can neither disprove nor prove the existence and influence of God. Individual scientists must be careful, therefore, not to go beyond their data and declare categorically that something does not exist just because they cannot observe it with their methods.

Turning to the second assumption of those clinicians

101

who criticize religion, it cannot be denied that religious truths are sometimes distorted by the faithful and used in ways that are psychologically damaging. Every counselor has seen people whose religion is enslaving and whose theological beliefs appear bizarre or nonsensical. But to conclude that the beliefs of emotionally disturbed people are typical of religious beliefs in general is to make a questionable generalization. As Walters has written,

> The inclusion of persons with defective reality testing is bound to give a distorted view of modal religious experience. The schizophrenic's impaired perception and...(thinking) does not bar him from participating in religious worship, but to incorporate the reports of his experience into a normative psychology of religion is comparable to treating the responses of the schizophrenic to questions about bodily functions as illuminating human physiology, or his comments on a meal as contributing to our understanding of nutrition.[18]

This, however, is exactly what many have done. William James, for example, made no attempt to distinguish normal from pathological views of religion. On the contrary, he assumed that a topic like religious experience would be best understood by studying its most pathological, "extreme...onesided, exaggerated, and intense" expressions.[19] Thus James's book is filled with illustrative case histories of people whose beliefs and experiences are unusual and atypical.

Freud made a similar mistake when he built his case against religion on subjective observations of neurotic people. Assuming that all religion was like that of his patients, he failed to observe or recognize that belief in the supernatural could be liberating and psychologically healthy. Freud and others also assumed that religious concepts in mental patients are a cause of the patient's problems. This is undoubtedly true in some cases but

102 such evidence gives us no basis to assume that all religion is harmful. Similarly, we should not conclude that all science is bad because some mental patients have been disturbed by reading science fiction books. Actually, religious beliefs and practice have been for many the cause of stability and psychological healing. Beliefs have helped these patients rather than hurt them.

What Freud and a number of like-minded people have done is to reject a caricature of religion without realizing what a mature religious faith is like or how it can influence an individual's life. Freud assumed that religion consisted primarily of guilt reactions, ritual, dogma, repressive rites, feelings of submission, and fear. He never seemed to realize that a religious system such as Christianity could be intellectually respectable and consistent with the facts of history, the conclusions of logicians, and even with the established facts of science. Neither Freud nor his followers seemed to realize that some of those who most strongly attack religion might have a naturalistic religion of their own. A case could be made that even psychoanalysis became a religion—that Freud was a high priest who demanded doctrinal orthodoxy from his followers and excommunicated those who dared question his conclusions. Today, some people make science their god. Others put faith in psychology, human potentiality, or some alternative system. Even scientific systems are built on presuppositions that are accepted by faith.

Within recent years a number of leaders in the field of clinical psychology have been concluding that religion might be a healthy influence after all.[20] Religion is being seen as something that should be encouraged or at least given serious consideration by psychologists, rather than being criticized, caricatured, minimized, or dismissed as being irrelevant or unimportant.

Of the three main forces in psychology, the humanists have been the most tolerant of religion. Because of their

103

interest in such issues as values, hope, inner experience, and the subjective meaning of life, third force psychologists have found themselves face to face with religious people who have some of the same concerns. There has been a willingness to study such things as prayer, meditation, or mystical insight and a realization that religion might even be able to increase our understanding of human thought and behavior.[21] Abraham Maslow wrote about ecstatic "peak experiences," and by the end of his life had begun thinking about what he called a *transhuman psychology.* Shortly before his death Maslow wrote:

> Immature though it yet is from a scientific point of view, humanistic psychology has already opened the doors to study of all those psychological phenomena which can be called transcendent or transpersonal, data which were closed off in principle by the inherent philosophical limitations of behaviorism and Freudianism. Among such phenomena I include not only higher and more positive states of consciousness and of personality...but also a conception of values (eternal verities) as part of a much-enlarged self.[22]

Maslow died before he was able to develop this transhuman psychology, but it seems likely that other third force psychologists will attempt to build on the foundational ideas that he laid.

When one reads the third force literature, however, one does not get the impression that psychologists in this movement have a widespread interest in religion. Although they acknowledge its importance and agree that perhaps it should be studied, humanistic psychologists for the most part either ignore religion, as do the behaviorists, or criticize it as do the clinicians. In a recent textbook on humanist psychology, the authors make reference to British educator, A. S. Neill, praise him for his dedication to humanism, and then with obvious

104   approval quote the following sentences from his
controversial book, *Summerhill:*

> The battle is not between believers in theology and
> non-believers in theology; it is between believers
> in human freedom and believers in the suppression
> of human freedom...some day a new generation
> will not accept the obsolete religion and myths of
> today. When the new religion comes, it will refute
> the idea of man's being born in sin. A new religion
> will praise God by making man happy.[23]

When third force psychologists write about religion,
they seem to be thinking about something subjective,
experiential, and dedicated to the praise and worship of
man and his potential. Neither third force nor transpersonal
psychology has much interest in a traditional theological
system like Christianity. At times one gets the impression
that humanism, like behaviorism and psychoanalysis, is
in itself a religious system: a religion for those who believe
in the innate goodness and optimistic future of man.

In the decade of the sixties when third force
psychology was getting its start, there appeared to be
considerable evidence for the demise of religion.
Attendance at religious services was steadily declining
and there was growing dissatisfaction with the seeming
irrelevance, internal squabbles, outmoded ritual, and
"establishment" image of the traditional church. Even
religious leaders like Bishop Robinson and Harvard
theologian Harvey Cox were urging people away from
fascination with mythology or belief in some supernatural
God who exists "up there" in the sky.[24] Some
theologians concluded, as Nietzsche had done many
years before, that God was dead. People were urged to
put their faith "in the possibilities of man," to develop the
love that was assumed to be innate in each individual,
and to turn their attention away from the mystical toward
more concrete attempts to solve the social problems of

105

our age. To help solve these problems, many people looked to science, especially social science; but it has become clear that even scientists are not able to transform mankind or solve the problems of society. People who have questions about the meaning of life and death, the basis for our values, or the destiny of man, find that science can give no answers. Thus, dissatisfied with the church and disillusioned with science, many people have developed a new interest in the supernatural, the mystical, and even the irrational. Widespread fascination with ESP, astrology, altered states of consciousness, Zen, eastern meditation, occultism, and mysterious new religions stands as a monument to humanity's deep-seated belief in and need to experience something beyond itself. Even within churches there is new interest in spontaneity, mystical experiences, glossolalia, koinonia groups and other experience-oriented activities. Freud's prediction that science would replace religion has not been fulfilled. Instead, even in the universities there is a return to what has been called "The Age of Unreason" and a "searching again for the sacred."[25]

It has been argued that everyone has some kind of religious system that guides behavior, affects thinking, and influences morals. We might prefer to call it a system of values or a philosophy of life, but it is still a system of beliefs about the world and oneself that has been accepted by faith. For some people these beliefs are clearly recognized, well-structured, and easily articulated; for others, the belief system is vague and rarely considered consciously. Many people evidently are content to go through life either not thinking much about their basic religious beliefs or uncritically accepting the nonrational religions of our day. Others (including, I would hope, most scientists) prefer to examine critically their own convictions and attitudes and eliminate those that don't make sense. They are willing to embrace new or altered beliefs, providing these are supported by impressive data, are capable of giving more meaning to one's personal life, and are better able to explain the details of human behavior.

To summarize our argument thus far, religion seems to have been largely ignored or explained away by the experimentalists, criticized by the clinicians, de-emphasized by the humanists, but recently embraced (especially in its nonrational forms) by increasing numbers of people. In one sense, all individuals believe in something, but psychologists as a whole have not given a lot of study to those beliefs[26] and how they influence the way in which scientists go about their work. Often religion is assumed to be in conflict with science, but it may be more accurate to conclude that the two fields complement each other. According to philosopher Arthur Holmes,[27] there are at least three ways in which the two fields interrelate.

First, religion and science both use models to explain reality. A model is a picture, analogy, or small copy of something that is too complicated to grasp directly. When the investigator works with a model, he is trying to simplify things by showing how a problem or object is like something with which we are familiar. A toy tractor, for example, could be thought of as a model of the real machine, a blueprint is a model of a larger house, the diagram of a football play is a model of the action on the field, and a mathematical formula could be a model of what happens when a chemical reaction occurs. Some models are simple; others are complex. Some models give an accurate picture of reality and other models are relatively inaccurate. In every case, however, a model is only a partial portrayal of reality. When we construct a model we try to select out the important elements of the problem or object and overlook everything else.

In psychology as with other branches of science various models have been proposed. Freud, for example, and a number of experimental researchers have used a biological model that pictures man as an animal. Gestalt psychology used a model borrowed from physics, Hull

107   and other learning theorists used mathematical models, and more recent behavioral scientists have used computer models that liken human behavior to a machine. All of these are attempts to simplify and help us to understand man's complexity.

The believer in religion also uses models to conceptualize and communicate ideas about spiritual reality. To describe God as a King, Judge, or Father is to tell something about his nature. To describe the relationship between deity and mankind in terms of the shepherd and sheep, the vine and the branches, or the hen and baby chickens is to use models or analogies that help us understand something about the God-man relationship.

Without the use of models the progress of science would have been much slower and the believer's understanding of God would have been more limited. There is always the danger, however, of taking the model too seriously and assuming that the model and the reality it represents are the same thing or that the model gives a complete picture of reality. To say that man is a machine or that Christ is a Rock[28] is to give a partial picture of what man and Christ are like. These pictures are not to be taken literally, nor are they meant to be a complete summary of all that we know about man or about Christ. To know about man we must use a variety of models—from chemistry, sociology, physiology, and the humanities, to name a few. To know about Christ, the Christian studies all of the parables, analogies, and word pictures in the Bible. Our understanding is always incomplete because our models are limited.

One of the reasons why science and religion have criticized each other is that each side fails to recognize or remember that the other uses models. When scientists (and some contemporary theologians) criticize religion for its symbolic language, they fail to realize that religious language is meant to give us a picture but not a literal description or complete portrayal of what a spiritual reality is like. Similarly, many psychologists would agree

108   that man is a responding organism. This is a picture, but
only one of many possible pictures, of what man is like.
A critic would be wrong if he assumed that most
psychologists believed that man is *nothing but* an
organism that responds to stimulation.

Any one event or phenomenon can usually be
explained on several different levels or from several
different viewpoints. Consider the experience of
religious conversion, for example. As with every other
human experience, conversion is a *biological* event
accompanied by minute but detectable changes in the
chemistry and physiological functioning of the
organism. It is a *psychological* event involving feelings,
thoughts, and behavioral changes. It is a *social*
phenomenon which may involve a decision in response
to social persuasion and a change in interpersonal
relations. It is a *philosophical* event involving an
individual's changing views of metaphysics. It is a
religious event involving one's relationship to God.

On each of these levels there could be extensive
analysis of the conversion experience. The psychologist,
for example, could give a "complete" psychological
explanation of the experience. This explanation might be
an accurate analysis of what happened psychologically
when the conversion occurred. But the psychological
explanation isn't the only explanation and doesn't say
everything there is to know about conversion. There can
also be accurate biological, sociological, philosophical,
and religious explanations of the same event. We can never
say, therefore, that conversion is *only* (nothing but) a
biological event, a psychological reaction, a social or
philosophical phenomenon, or a change in theology. To
try to understand a human event like conversion we must
see it from a variety of viewpoints. To expect that a
human being can be fully analyzed by only one of these
viewpoints is to oversimplify man and limit our ability to
understand, predict, and control behavior.[29]

A second thing that Holmes points out about the
relationship between science and religion is that the

109 conflict is not ultimately over empirical facts, important as these are, but between the a *priori* principles or assumptions upon which the facts and models are built. As we have seen, the scientific psychologist and the theologian tend to view an event from different perspectives. Science and theology are concerned with different facts (and often different issues) and they describe their findings in different terms. The theologian would never use operational definitions or describe the statistical probability of an event, but neither would the scientist use the figurative language of, say, the last book in the Bible. In his work the scientist seeks to give precise descriptions of a limited body of data, but the theologian, who also seeks for precision, nevertheless tends to use more picturesque and metaphorical terms to comprehend God and his creation. The scientist and the theologian might disagree over behaviorism, mechanistic determinism, or the irrelevance of religion, but this is a conflict not so much over empirical facts as over the presuppositions that guide one's data-gathering and interpretation of facts.

In reading this chapter some readers may have been wondering why a book that began as a reexamination of psychology has begun to talk more and more about religion. This, as Holmes states in his third conclusion, is because science and every other human endeavor find their ultimate meaning in religion. We have maintained that every psychologist (and every nonpsychologist) has a set of presuppositions that molds what he studies, the way in which he conducts investigations, and the meaning he gives to his data. Since these foundational assumptions cannot be proven conclusively with empirical methods, they must come from some place other than science. There may seem to be a variety of potential world views underlying psychology, but according to Holmes, there really can be only two sources from which a scientist's presuppositions can be drawn: theism, which involves belief in God, or nontheistic naturalism. The scientist's world view must be

110   horizontal, dealing only with man and making no
reference to God; or it must be vertical, based on a
theistic system which, while concerned about man and
interested in natural phenomena, also acknowledges at
least the probable existence of a Divine Being.

Footnotes
Chapter 6

[1]James, William. *The Varieties of Religious Experience,* Garden City,
N.Y.: Doubleday, 1902; Freud, S., *The Future of an Illusion,* Garden
City, N.Y.: Doubleday, 1927; Allport, Gordon, *The Individual and His
Religion,* New York: MacMillan, 1950. There are, of course, a
number of psychologists who are interested in religion. Many belong
to organizations such as the Christian Association for Psychological
Studies, Psychologists Interested in Religious Issues (a division of the
American Psychological Association), or the Academy of Religion
and Mental Health. Many psychologists publish papers in journals
such as *The Journal of Psychology and Theology, The Journal for the
Scientific Study of Religion,* or *The Journal of the American Scientific
Affiliation.* In spite of this activity, however, the psychological study
of religion has remained on the fringes of psychology and has been of
interest to only a minority of psychologists.
[2]Russell, Bertrand. *Why I Am Not a Christian.* New York: Simon &
Schuster, 1957.
[3]Harris, George T. "The B. F. Skinner Manifesto: All the World's a Box,"
Psychology Today, August 1971, pp. 33-35.
[4]Skinner, B. F. *Science and Human Behavior.* New York: MacMillan,
1953, chapter 23, "Religion."
[5]James, *op. cit.*
[6]See, for example, Beit-Hallahmi, Benjamin, *Research in Religious
Behavior: Selected Readings,* Monterey, California: Brooks/Cole, 1973,
and Brown, L. B. (ed.), *Psychology and Religion: Selected Readings,*
Baltimore: Penguin, 1973.
[7]Thouless, Robert H. *An Introduction to the Psychology of Religion*
(3rd ed.). Cambridge: Cambridge University Press, 1971, p. 5.
[8]Ellis, Albert. *Humanistic Psychotherapy: The Rational Emotive
Approach.* New York: Julian Press, 1973; see also Ellis's papers
"There Is No Place for the Concept of Sin in Psychotherapy,"
Journal of Counseling Psychology 7, 1960, pp. 188-192, and "The Case
Against Religion: A Psychotherapist's View," *Mensa Bulletin,*
September 1970, No. 28, pp. 5, 6.
[9]During the summer of 1971, Freud's consultation room, waiting
room, and office in Vienna were converted into a museum. Among the
items displayed are photographs of Freud's working area. Several of
these photographs show the religious objects that surrounded Freud
while he wrote his many papers and books.
[10]Among the best known of Freud's works on religion are *Totem and
Taboo* (first published in 1913), London: Routledge & Kegan Paul,
1961; *The Future of an Illusion* (first published in 1927), *op. cit.;* and
Moses and Monotheism (first published in 1939), London: Hogarth
Press (volume 23) 1964.

[11]Lubin, A. J. "A Psychoanalytic View of Religion." In M. Pattison (ed.), *Clinical Psychiatry and Religion,* Boston: Little, Brown, and Company, 1969, pp. 49-60.

[12]Freud, S. *Totem and Taboo. op. cit.,* pp. 147, 148.

[13]Freud, S. *Civilization and Its Discontents.* London: Hogarth Press, 1939, p. 23.

[14]Freud, S. *Leonardo da Vinci.* London: Kegan Paul, 1932, p. 103.

[15]Freud, S. *The Future of an Illusion, op. cit.,* pp. 54, 29, 61, 77-8, 87, 97.

[16]*Ibid.,* p. 96.

[17]Walters, Orville S. "Dubious Psychiatry: A Review of 'Religion May Be Hazardous to Your Health,' by Eli S. Chesen," *Christianity Today,* February 16, 1973, pp. 497-8.

[18]Walters, Orville S. "Religion and Psychopathology," *Comprehensive Psychiatry* **101,** 1964, pp. 24-35.

[19]James, *op. cit.,* pp. 44, 49.

[20]See, for example, Allport, *op. cit.;* Mowrer, O. H., *The Crisis in Psychiatry and Religion,* Princeton: Van Nostrand, 1961; and Meehl, P., et al., *What, Then, Is Man?,* St. Louis: Concordia, 1958; also, footnote 1.

[21]See, for example, the quotation by Bugental on pages 65 and 66 of this book.

[22]Maslow, A. H. *Motivation and Personality* (2nd ed.). New York: Harper & Row, 1970, p. xxvii.

[23]Buhler, C., & Allen, M. *Introduction to Humanistic Psychology.* Monterey, California: Brooks/Cole, 1972, p. 95.

[24]Robinson, John A. T. *Honest To God.* Philadelphia: Westminster, 1963; Cox, Harvey, *The Secular City* (rev. ed.), New York: MacMillan, 1965.

[25]These terms were used in a series of *Time* magazine articles (see "The New Cult of Madness: Thinking as a Bad Habit," March 13, 1972, pp. 27-30; and a series entitled "Second Thoughts About Man," April 2, 9, 16, 23, 1973). See also *The Religious Reawakening in America,* Washington: U. S. News and World Report books, 1972.

[26]The work of Rokeach and others is very important but is not focused primarily on how the scientist's belief system influences his work (see Rokeach, Milton, *The Open and Closed Mind,* New York: Basic Books, 1960; *Beliefs, Attitudes and Values,* San Francisco: Jossey-Bass, 1968).

[27]Holmes, A. F. *Faith Seeks Understanding.* Grand Rapids: Eerdmans, 1971, pp. 29-34.

[28]In 1 Corinthians 10:4, Christ is referred to as a Rock. For a fuller discussion of man as a complex machine, see the *Journal of the American Scientific Affiliation,* December 1970. For a fuller discussion of models in science and religion, see Jeeves, Malcolm A., *The Scientific Enterprise and Christian Faith,* Downers Grove, Illinois: Inter-Varsity, 1969, Chapter 4.

[29]Jeeves, *ibid.;* Bube, Richard H., *The Human Quest,* Waco, Texas: Word, 1971; see also Skinner, B. F., "The Machine That is Man," *Psychology Today* **2,** April 1969, p. 25f.

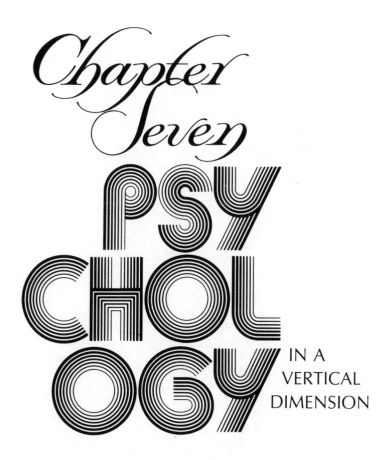

Chapter Seven

PSYCHOLOGY
IN A VERTICAL DIMENSION

IN the preceding pages we have argued that psychology is in a dilemma. Popular among college students and growing as a profession, it has nevertheless tended to become fragmented, overspecialized, and irrelevant. Within the profession are those who recognize the problems and who are working to improve psychology, but we have suggested that the improvement needed is at a deep level. Psychologists or psychology students must reexamine and be willing to alter, if necessary, the philosophical foundations on which their science is built.

The empiricist might wish that he could use psychological research methods to discover objectively a world view and set of usable assumptions, but presuppositions are not chosen that way.[1] On the contrary, assumptions about man and the universe tend to be developed subjectively. They come before the research ever begins and they direct the kind of investigations that are subsequently done.

Since one can never be without subjective assumptions it has been proposed that the psychologist should at least acknowledge and clarify the assumptions that guide his work.[2] But we can go further than this. Even though our presuppositions cannot be empirically arrived at nor experimentally proven, they can still be examined critically. By examination we can discover that some assumptions are more logical than others, are capable of producing more fruitful research, are better able to help us make sense of our data, and are more consistent with what we have learned about the universe from other sources.

Imagine, for example, that back in history psychology's founding fathers had decided one day to select the assumptions on which their discipline would be built. At a meeting to discuss the issue, somebody might raise the question of whether psychology should build on the assumption of empiricism (the idea that scientifically derived facts are the only source of truth) or whether the discipline should assume that knowledge comes from a variety of sources (including, let us say, empirically derived facts, logical deduction, and divine revelation). Here is the issue of epistemology: the problem of the source of knowledge. The people at the meeting might choose to flip a coin in order to decide which of their assumptions would be best, or perhaps they might take a vote to discover the subjective preferences of those in the room. Wouldn't it make better sense, however, to examine critically the different alternatives in an attempt to determine which was more logical, which would lead to more information about human behavior, and which had potential for producing clearer explanations of why people act as they do? It might even be that some already-existing data would tend to support one alternative rather than the other.

Assumptions, as we have seen, are very important—too important to be ignored as in the past, selected unconsciously, or chosen on the basis of vague subjective feelings. Assumptions give us a point of view for looking at the world. They are at the basis of every observation, every argument, every scientific endeavor, every interpretation of facts, and every conclusion. It would seem desirable, however, to have as few presuppositions as possible and to incorporate a minimum of content in the assumptions that we do have.[3] When our list of assumptions grows and gets more detailed, we become more bound by them, less free to investigate the world, and less able to discover what is true or false. The scientist's goal, therefore, is to assume as little as is necessary and to accept assumptions that are concise, logical, coherent, consistent with each other, and supported by the facts of experience.

In this chapter and the one that follows I would like to present evidence in support of the unconventional suggestion that it is most logical to build psychology on a religious foundation, and specifically on a presuppositional base derived from and in accordance with the teachings of the Bible.

At this point I risk losing some of my readers. Most

psychologists probably will admit that the assumptions on which their science is built may be in need of revision. Many will concede that traditional psychological criticisms of religion are unfounded or distorted and that religious beliefs might even be a good thing for mankind. On first glance, however, it is much more difficult to go one step further and accept the proposal that religious assumptions, and specifically biblically-based assumptions, should provide the foundation on which psychology should be rebuilt. But before people reject the proposed biblical foundation for psychology, they should at least examine what this foundation might be like and should consider the supporting evidence.

John Warwick Montgomery tells a story about the unwillingness of some people to accept evidence that goes against their preconceived conclusions.

> Once upon a time there was a man who thought he was dead. His concerned wife and friends sent him to the friendly neighborhood psychiatrist. The psychiatrist determined to cure him by convincing him of one fact that contradicted his belief that he was dead. The psychiatrist decided to use the simple truth that dead men do not bleed. He put his patient to work reading medical texts, observing autopsies, etc. After weeks of effort, the patient finally said, "All right, all right! You've convinced me. Dead men do not bleed." Whereupon the psychiatrist stuck him in the arm with a needle, and the blood flowed. The man looked down with a contorted, ashen face and cried: "Good Lord! Dead men bleed after all!"
>
> This parable illustrates that if you hold unsound presuppositions with sufficient tenacity, facts will make no difference at all, and you will be able to create a world of your own, totally unrelated to reality and totally incapable of being touched by reality. Such a condition (which the philosophers call solipsistic, which psychiatrists call autistically

psychotic, and which lawyers call insane) is tantamount to death because connection with the living world is severed. The man in the parable not only thought he was dead, but in a very real sense, he *was* dead because facts no longer meant anything to him.[4]

In spite of some popular beliefs to the contrary, psychologists and their students are not out of contact with reality. Most do not have much interest in religion and many will be surprised to read that someone would seriously propose that psychology should be recast "in a vertical dimension"—looking upward to God. But there is within psychology at least an expressed willingness to consider facts and arguments even when these contradict more generally accepted beliefs and presuppositions about man and his behavior.

Let us consider the suggestion that, in the future, psychology could be more productive and less in a dilemma if it were built on the major premise that God exists and is the source of all truth. This assumption could serve as a starting point from which data could be collected, systems could be built, therapy could be developed, and principles of living could be derived. It is offered in place of the currently accepted assumption that God is nonexistent and that there is no deity who has anything to do with truth. In a sense both assumptions are theological. The first says God exists; the second says he does not exist.

The assumption that God exists and is the source of all truth is not, however, a completely arbitrary assumption. It is not something "pulled out of the air" and decreed by fiat as being true. On the contrary, there is good evidence for accepting this premise. Such evidence cannot conclusively prove the premise, but I think it can show this assumption to be a better starting place for psychology than is the alternative assumption of God's nonexistence.

119   Throughout history attempts have been made to prove the existence of God. Thomas Aquinas, for example, looked at the natural world and concluded that there must be a prime mover for everything, a first cause for all subsequent events, a sustainer holding everything together, a perfect being imposing perfection on the world, and a controlling being giving the world order. "Look around you," Aquinas said, in essence. "This can't all have come about by chance; there must be a God." Later philosophers like Kant demolished all such arguments and showed that neither God's existence nor his nonexistence can be proven logically, at least with the precision of a mathematical proof.[5] Other writers then argued from religious experience. Pascal, for example, suggested that "the heart has its reasons which reason does not know," and William James, the psychologist-turned-philosopher, wrote that "I myself believe that evidence for God lies primarily in inner personal experience."[6] But personal experience is a shaky foundation on which to build any argument. It cannot be checked by others, it is difficult to describe precisely, and it can result in as many different "gods" as there are feelings or individuals with religious experience.

Even if rational deduction and subjective experience could prove God's existence, the research-oriented psychologist might still want a different kind of proof: empirical data that he and all others could observe. Such data is available and some of it will be summarized in the next chapter, but even such data cannot prove categorically that God exists. As in every other scientific investigation, the observation of empirical evidence can at best determine the probability of God's existence. When we limit our investigation to use of the scientific method, we can never be 100 percent certain of God's existence or of anything else.

None of this is surprising if we realize that God, by definition, is a supreme Being who is greater than all of the methods—rational, experiential, or empirical—that we might use in an attempt to demonstrate his existence.

120

> There is nothing greater by which men can attempt to demonstrate the existence of God. If there were, He would not be God or men's final answer to the questions regarding reality. That God *is*, while it can be rendered probable, cannot be demonstrated "absolutely" by empirical data....Hence, all science, including psychology—using all the means of human perception for inquiries which are determined by the utmost methodological rigor—cannot possibly provide us with proofs or exhaustive explanations of God.[7]

Even though there is no adequate way to prove with certainty that God exists, neither is there conclusive proof of his nonexistence. Of the two alternatives, however, only the assumption that God exists gives a rationale for order in the universe and an explanation for the purpose, dignity, and destiny of man—who is, after all, the prime subject matter of psychology.

A non-Christian psychologist might be willing to agree that belief in the existence of God is at least as plausible as belief in his nonexistence, but the second part of our major premise—that God is the source of all truth—may be more difficult for him to accept. The question of truth, however, is at the core of the intellectual and scientific enterprise. The source of knowledge and the means of acquiring knowledge are at the basis of most disagreements between psychology and Christianity or between psychology and the other sciences. This epistemological issue also is central to disagreements among the experimental, applied-clinical, and humanistic branches within psychology.

To begin our discussion of the second half of the major premise we should consider briefly the word *truth*. As traditionally used in philosophy, truth implies an abstract idea, a universal reality that exists and can be grasped by analysis or experimentation.[8] Psychologists have always found this concept difficult to accept and have preferred to avoid the word altogether. When we do encounter the word, we have been inclined to define it as "an accurate picture of the world as it really is." The only way to get an accurate picture is to accumulate evidence and to assume that the greater the evidence and the greater the consensus about what the evidence means, then the closer we are to possession of the truth.

Unlike the psychologist, the Christian presupposes that truth is found not so much in an abstract idea or in a scientific consensus as in a person. God *is* truth and it is from him that all truth springs. Truth is assumed to come from God to man in two ways which theologians call general revelation and special revelation. *General revelation,* sometimes called natural revelation, refers to the truths that God has revealed through nature, science, or history; and which man can know by observation, empirical investigation, logical deduction, intuition, feeling, the study of tradition, or any other technique apart from reading the Bible. The body of knowledge that comes through these means is incomplete, limited by such things as inadequate methodology, biased perceptions, or inability to comprehend. It is the purpose of all science, including psychology, to study carefully what God has revealed through nature and to attain a better understanding of the universe and its operation. From the Christian's perspective, all truth comes from God, and all seekers, whether theists or not, are searching for truth which is of divine origin.

Might it be, however, that there are some truths which man cannot grasp on his own; some phenomena which cannot be observed or deduced by the techniques we have at our disposal? If we assume the existence of an infinite God, for example, then surely we who are finite can have no conception on our own of what that God is like. We can never know if there is purpose in life or meaning to history, if there is hope for an afterlife, or if there are any absolute standards of right or wrong. For answers to these and similar questions many people look to the Bible, a book that Christians believe to be God's written

122   or *special revelation* to man. In the Bible, for example, we read about Jesus Christ and discover things about him that we would never have known otherwise: that he is God's Son but equal with the Father, that Christ created all things, that he came to earth to show us what God is like, that all truth comes to man through him, that he was crucified and rose again in order to make salvation possible for sinful human beings, and that belief in him is the only way to approach God.[9] The Bible records something of God's intervention in history, it gives us a glimpse of what God is like, and it shows how we can know God in a personally meaningful way. Although our understanding of the Bible may be limited and subject to human misinterpretation, men and women nevertheless continue to study this book in an attempt to understand its message. The Bible is regarded by Christians as a trustworthy and completed book, given to us by God through the efforts of morally upright individuals who were divinely guided as they wrote.[10]

But why should the Bible be set up as any kind of authority? Wouldn't it be just as logical to assume that God's special revelation, if there is such a thing, came through the Koran, the words of Plato, the experience of transcendental meditation, the visions of medieval and modern mystics, or even the writings of chairman Mao Tse-tung? Just because the Bible claims to be God's Word is no proof of its authority, since many men and women, including a lot of psychotics, have claimed to have special revelations from God. Clearly, if we are going to accept any kind of revealed truth we should accept whatever revelation best fits the facts of history and conclusions of established science, has the greatest internal consistency, gives the most complete explanation of the "unknown" and otherwise unknowable things about life (such as the nature of man or the meaning of life), and has the fewest translation inaccuracies or obvious errors. Many competent scholars are convinced that the Bible best fits these standards, and in the following pages we will mention some of their arguments.[11]

123   However, why should we worry about revelation at all? How could it have any bearing on psychology? Why don't we just stick with the "facts" we discover through modern science and forget the message of a controversial and ancient book? This is what Skinner would propose and it is likely that Freud would have agreed.[12] As we have seen, however, facts cannot be observed or interpreted in a vacuum, without guiding assumptions, and we propose that a divine revelation enables the scientist to have an understanding, a hope, and an open-mindedness that he would not have otherwise. Let us consider each of these in turn.

First, divine revelation gives us understanding. Viktor Frankl, the well-known psychiatrist, has written persuasively about modern man's need to find meaning and purpose in life,[13] but as Frankl and many others have pointed out, millions of people today have not found this meaning. Their lives are empty, and in spite of excessive busyness, they realize that human existence is largely futile, "full of sound and fury but signifying nothing." Samuel Becket has poignantly expressed this in *Waiting for Godot.*

> We wait. We are bored. (He throws up his hand). No, don't protest, we are bored to death, there's no denying it. Good. A diversion comes along and what do we do? We let it go to waste. Come, let's get to work! (He advances towards the heap, stops in his stride.) In an instant all will vanish and we'll be alone once more, in the midst of nothingness.

A sense of futility permeates the whole society but is seen with special clarity in the universities, including the departments of psychology. Students and professors spend their time accumulating what Gordon Allport has termed "an array of itty bitty facts,"[14] but there is no unifying principle that can pull everything together into a coherent world view. The scientist or student who thinks much about his academic work is often left with a feeling

124   of confusion, skepticism, and sometimes despair. Little
wonder that many people conclude that "thinking is a bad
habit" or that "nothing makes sense" anymore.[15]

But the Bible enables us to make sense of a lot that
would otherwise be confusing. For one thing the Bible
gives an overview, many would say a divine perspective, of
history which lets the events of our times be seen in a
broader context. If we assume, as the Bible states, that a
supreme God created, sustains, and has plans for the
universe, including individual human beings and nations,
then there is less cause for despair, worry, and
frustration.[16] The Bible also gives us a reason for believing
that the world is orderly. Science assumes this, but
science cannot account for regularity or have any
assurance that the world which is orderly today will be
orderly tomorrow. All that science actually observes in
nature, writes Carnell, "is a sequence of regularity; but
this regularity is compatible with either Christianity, where
God (who exists and has revealed himself) keeps it
regular, or with blind naturalism where (goodness knows
what!) keeps it regular."[17] With its emphasis on the
supernatural, the Bible can give us a perspective for
understanding so-called miracles, occult phenomena,
extrasensory perception, and religious experience. Of
more interest to the psychologist, perhaps, is the Bible's
unifying philosophy of man: he was created in God's
image, was given the freedom to rebel (which he did), is
sustained by divine power, is valued by God, has the
freedom to accept or reject God's gift of salvation, and
has an eternal destiny.[18] In addition, the Bible's perspective
on such issues as love, anger, marriage, human rights,
ethics, or the importance of childhood[19] could shed some
light on human behavior that we might not have
discovered elsewhere.

Besides understanding, the divine revelation gives a
hope that we would otherwise not have. Many years ago
Søren Kierkegaard, the Danish philosopher, concluded
that reasoning was of limited value and that man had to
make a blind "leap of faith" into the unknown. Some

125   writers believe that acceptance of this philosophy was one of the early reasons for man's moving into the present state of anti-intellectualism and despair.[20] The Bible, however, does not promulgate a "leap of faith" philosophy. It demonstrates and promises God's forgiveness, guidance, protection, help, love, faithfulness, power, and mercy. It enables the believer not to plunge into the dark, but to put his hope confidently in something that is clearly spelled out. For the Christian, faith is not an irrational jump into an abyss; it is a complete dependence on a dependable and trustworthy God who has revealed himself to humankind.

Third, the divine revelation gives us an open-mindedness that we would otherwise not have. Often it is assumed that the believer in divine revelation is restricted by the Bible and unwilling to consider any facts that don't fit his preconceived world view. As psychologist Malcolm Jeeves has shown, however, it is the *non*believer who is the narrow thinker. Both the theist and the non-theist start with a set of presuppositions, but the Christian viewpoint

> ...is more open-minded in that in the first place it agrees that it is perfectly legitimate to assume uniformity in nature, but at the same time it is willing to entertain the possibility of miracle, if there are found to be good historical grounds for doing so....The theist is found to be more open-minded towards the historical material than the non-theist who must, because of his presuppositions, do his utmost to explain away the historicity of the record of any events which do not fit with his presuppositions.[21]

That God exists and is the source of all truth is the major premise we need on which to build a science or other field of inquiry. All knowledge derives from this presupposition and every conclusion ultimately rests on it. There is, however, a corollary presupposition which

126 grows out of the first and is of great importance to psychology. This is the assumption that *man who exists is able to know the truth*.

Most psychologists are familiar with Descartes' famous *cogito ergo sum* (I think; therefore I am), but probably few of us have much interest in philosophical arguments about whether or not man really does exist. It seems more important to be concerned about problems of loneliness, discouragement, lack of meaning, frustration, and human impotence in the face of widespread social turmoil. If he does stop to ponder human existence, the psychologist, especially the clinician, is more likely to conclude that "I feel and behave; therefore I must exist."

The Bible gives a more complete description of man's existence and even says something both about his ability to know the truth and about his problems. Man, we read, was created by God and was in many respects made like God "in the divine image." The Creator did not make us into robots. Instead, he gave us freedom to run our own lives, but we have used this freedom to deny and rebel against him. Such denial and rebellion are what the Bible calls sin and are at the basis of man's social problems. Happily for us, God sent Jesus Christ to the earth to show us how to live, to defeat sin by his atoning death on the cross, and to give believers assurance of continued personal existence after death. The Bible phrases it this way:

> Jesus said, "I am the way, and the truth, and the life; no one comes to the Father, but through Me...For God so loved the world, that He gave His only begotten Son, that whoever believes in Him should not perish, but have eternal life. For God did not send the Son into the world to judge the world; but that the world should be saved through Him. He who believes in Him is not judged; he who does not believe has been judged already, because he has not believed in the name of the only begotten Son of God...He who believes in the Son has eternal life;

127

but he who does not obey the Son shall not see life, but the wrath of God abides on him.''[22]

To the Christian these words make perfectly good sense but to the nonbeliever all of this may at first glance seem like foolishness. Can it possibly be true that Jesus Christ makes personal immortality possible, or that events after death are really dependent on the beliefs and presuppositions that we accept here on earth? This is a conclusion we could never discover through science or through logical deduction. God had to reveal it and it is only because of him that we can know it.

In talking to some of his followers Jesus once commented about the ability of individuals to come to conclusions such as those discussed above. ''You must continually study my Word, the Bible,'' he said in essence. It is then that ''you shall know the truth and the truth shall make you free.''[23] The Bible teaches that God's Holy Spirit guides people in their study and helps them to know the truth.[24] This is not to imply that the person who ignores the Bible will never discover any truth. Such a conclusion would be untenable; there are innumerable non-Christian scientists who are discovering some aspect of truth every day. Of course these investigators also reach erroneous conclusions and for this reason scientists are constantly repeating their observations and testing their findings against other findings known to have high probability of being valid. The Christian believes, however, that the Bible provides another standard against which to test our conclusions.

It should not be assumed that the Christian who accepts the Bible's reliability can then claim always to have the truth and to be free from error. In spite of their best intentions, all people make mistakes, misinterpret data, and reach conclusions that subsequently are found to be wrong. The reasons for human misinterpretation are well known: bias or miscalculation in our observations or deductions, lack of suitable observation or measuring techniques, inability to collect all of the relevant data, etc.

128 In addition, man himself is limited. He has a finite mind which even with the aid of computers cannot comprehend all of the mysteries of the universe. The Christian believes, further, that God has not chosen to reveal all of truth to man, and even the truth available cannot be perceived without distortion because man is an imperfect (sinful) creature.

According to the Bible, error in our thinking also arises from the existence and influence of satanic forces. Prior to the recent upsurge of interest in occultism and Satan worship, the devil was pretty much dismissed as a myth. His actual existence was rarely taken seriously. Even today the devil and his nature almost never get mentioned in psychology textbooks (or in many theology textbooks, for that matter). As one psychologist has observed, however, "In contemporary society, the strongest assistance to Satan's work is the denial of his existence, for the greatest enemy is the unknown enemy."[25] One is reminded of the oft-quoted comment of C. S. Lewis, that "there are two equal and opposite errors into which our race can fall about the devils. One is to disbelieve in their existence. The other is to believe, and to feel an excessive and unhealthy interest in them."[26] Rather than actively believing or disbelieving, it would seem that most people simply ignore the possibility of satanic influence. The devil's existence can no more be proven logically and empirically than can the existence of God. We learn of Satan only through the warnings that come from God through divine revelation. "Be of sober spirit," we read, "be on the alert. Your adversary, the devil, prowls around like a roaring lion seeking someone to devour. But resist him, be firm in your faith...Resist the devil and he will flee from you. Draw near to God." The devil is described as the "father of lies" who "does not stand in the truth, because there is no truth in him. Whenever he speaks a lie, he speaks from his own nature; for he is a liar."[27] To believe in the devil is to believe in the possibility of satanically-produced error creeping into our work and masquerading as truth.

129

Figure 1:
The Source of knowledge
God exists and is the source of all truth. This truth comes to us in two ways: by special revelation (that which is recorded in the Bible), and by general revelation (that which comes to man by way of science, logic, insight, tradition, perception, etc.). Man, who also exists, is able to know the truth, but he has the challenge of interpreting what is revealed and distinguishing truth from error. This diagram is discussed further in the text.

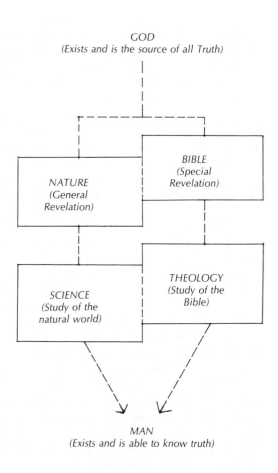

GOD
(Exists and is the source of all Truth)

NATURE
(General Revelation)

BIBLE
(Special Revelation)

SCIENCE
(Study of the natural world)

THEOLOGY
(Study of the Bible)

MAN
(Exists and is able to know truth)

Figure 1 summarizes what we have concluded thus far about the new foundation that we believe must be the basis for psychology. God exists and all truth comes from him by way of the Bible (special revelation) or by nature (general revelation). Man, who exists, is able to know the truth, which comes through theology (the systematic study and interpretation of the Bible) and through science, broadly defined to include empirical observation, logical deduction, and studies of

130   humanities (the systematic study and interpretation of the world in which we live). It is not to be assumed that the study of God's general revelation is either less or more honorable than the study of his special revelation. All truth comes from God, so the search for truth is a noble endeavor whether one searches in the Bible, in the laboratory, in the library, or in the counselor's office. The biblical revelation, as we have seen, provides insight into the nature of man and his world, but science also clarifies and illuminates many of the truths of the Bible. Peter's denial of Jesus may be viewed by some Bible students as Satan inspired, but the psychologist could view it as a psychological reaction to fear. We do not say that either of these interpretations is more correct or informative than the other. They both increase our understanding of behavior under stress.

It should not be assumed, however, that biblical and natural revelation are of equal validity. The biblical revelation has a higher priority (which we have tried to illustrate by raising the right side of the diagram in Figure 1).[28] It deals with ultimate meaning, makes known God's nature and works, describes supernatural forces, gives a reason for believing in the dignity of man and the orderliness of the universe, informs us of man's destiny and the divine plan of salvation, instructs us concerning God's ethical standards, and gives us the divine perspective on history. All of this is not only beyond the realm of science but gives a structure into which the facts and methods of science can fit.

If one accepts the major premise of this chapter (that God exists and is the source of all truth which he reveals through special and general revelation), then one has more data with which to work than does the investigator who disbelieves in God or who ignores the Bible. The majority of psychologists confine their activities to the left side of Figure 1. They study only behavior, restrict themselves to the use of empirical methods, and ignore the facts of special revelation. The secular psychologist has created difficulties for himself because he has focused exclusively on one part of the diagram: that labeled "general revelation," "science," and "man."

In a similar way, some theologians have restricted themselves to a study of special revelation and, by ignoring the world around them, have tended to drift into irrelevance. But the theologian needs to understand science and natural revelation almost as much as the scientist needs to study biblical revelation. "The scientist may locate the facts, but he cannot make them stick together without the pattern of the mind of Christ; and Christianity, while it may be self-consistent, cannot enjoy perfect tangency to the data of nature until it relates its system to the empirical data of science. In union there is strength; in diversion there is weakness."[29]

The psychologist who accepts the premise that God exists and is the source of truth must take a somewhat different approach to his subject matter. First, like every other psychologist he must strive for as good an understanding of the natural world as possible. This means that he must be a competent researcher who uses his skills to discover what he can about the natural world. Second, he must have as good an understanding of specific revelation as possible. This means that he must be a diligent student of the Bible who knows its teachings and seeks continually to understand its contents. Third, the psychologist must continually test his scientifically derived facts against the revealed truths of the Bible. Sometimes, of course, this will not be a very important part of his work. The researcher who studies synapses in the brain or the conditioned behavior of pigeons is working in an area that the Bible never discusses. When we begin to interpret data, however, we must at least be alert to biblical teaching. Unlike many other sciences, psychology is primarily concerned with the behavior of man. Since this topic is also dealt with extensively in the Bible, the psychologist and theologian frequently find themselves dealing with the same subject matter. When conflicts arise, more data need to be collected, but ultimately, since the Bible has priority, Christianity and

132 science are harmonized not by testing the Bible against science but by testing science against the Bible.

If we accept the fact that God exists and is the source of all truth we must recognize that he does not contradict himself. Thus the truths that come via special revelation and the truths of general revelation cannot contradict each other. The contents of the Bible and the valid conclusions of science must be in perfect harmony. If they are not, then some of our facts or our interpretations are wrong. Either we have uncovered error in our scientific endeavors or we have misinterpreted the Bible, or both. The scientist who is a Christian must seek to bring these two bodies of knowledge into harmony—not by stretching data and forcing facts, but by further study and attempts to obtain clearer, more accurate data. In the future, as so often in the past, we will discover that God's Word and God's world are in perfect harmony.

Footnotes
Chapter 7

[1]VanKaam, Adrian. "Assumptions in Psychology," *Journal of Individual Psychology* **14**, 1958, pp. 22-28.

[2]*Ibid.* See also Giorgi, Amedeo, *Psychology as a Human Science,* New York: Harper & Row, 1970; and Hudson, Liam, *The Cult of the Fact,* London: Jonathan Cape, 1972.

[3]Montgomery, J. W. *The Shape of the Past.* Ann Arbor: Edwards, 1962.

[4]Montgomery, J. W. *The Altizer-Montgomery Dialogue.* Downers Grove, Illinois: Inter-Varsity, 1967, p. 21f.

[5]Plantinga, Alvin. *God and Other Minds.* Ithaca, N. Y.: Cornell University Press, 1967.

[6]Carnell, Edward J. *An Introduction to Christian Apologetics.* Grand Rapids, Michigan: Eerdmans, 1948, p. 74-5.

[7]Meehl, P., *et al. What, Then, Is Man?* St. Louis: Concordia, 1958, p. 25.

[8]Bloesch, Donald. *The Ground of Certainty.* Grand Rapids: Eerdmans, 1971, p. 128.

[9]See the Bible, Philippians 2:5, 6; John 10:30; Colossians 1:16, 2:3; Romans 5:9; 1 Peter 1:3; John 3:16, 6:47, 11:25, 12:45, 14:6-10.

[10]2 Timothy 3:16; 2 Peter 1:21.

[11]For more complete and systematic discussions of the Bible's validity, see Carnell, *op. cit.,* chapter 11, and Pinnock, Clark H., *Set Forth Your Case: An Examination of Christianity's Credentials,* Chicago: Moody, 1967, chapter 12. Bruce, F. F., *The New Testament Documents: Are They Reliable?,* Grand Rapids: Eerdmans, 1959, is a longer but readable treatment of the topic. More popular is a symposium, Clark, Gordon H., *et al., Can I Trust My Bible?,* Chicago: Moody, 1963, and Tenney, M. C. (ed.), *The Bible: The Living Word of Revelation,* Grand Rapids: Zondervan, 1968. All of the above are available in inexpensive

133

paperback editions. For a more complete and scholarly treatment see Pinnock, Clark H., *Biblical Revelation: The Foundation of Christian Theology,* Chicago: Moody, 1971.

[12]Skinner, B. F. *Science and Human Behavior.* New York: MacMillan, 1953; Freud, S., "Instincts and Their Vicissitudes," in *Collected Papers,* Vol. III, London: Hogarth Press, 1925, pp. 60-83.

[13]Frankl, V. E. *Man's Search for Meaning: An Introduction to Logotherapy.* New York: Washington Square Press, 1959.

[14]Allport, Gordon W. "The Person in Psychology," in F. T. Severin (ed.), *Humanistic Viewpoints in Psychology,* New York: McGraw-Hill, 1965, pp. 34-47.

[15]Maddocks, Melvin. "The New Cult of Madness: Thinking as a Bad Habit," *Time,* March 13, 1972, pp. 27-30.

[16]See Montgomery, J. W. *Where Is History Going?* Grand Rapids: Zondervan, 1969.

[17]Carnell, *op. cit.,* p. 234.

[18]Genesis 1:26, 27; Romans 3:23, 6:23; Colossians 1:15, 16; John 3:16; 1 John 1:8, 9; Ephesians 2:8, 9; Hebrews 9:27; Romans 1:18.

[19]1 Corinthians 13; Ephesians 4:26; Proverbs 15:1, 18; Ephesians 5:24-26; Proverbs 22:2, 6; Romans 10:12; 1 Timothy 6:1-12; Titus 2:12, etc.

[20]Schaeffer, Francis A. *The God Who Is There.* Chicago: Inter-Varsity, 1968.

[21]Jeeves, Malcolm A. *The Scientific Enterprise and Christian Faith.* Downers Grove, Illinois: Inter-Varsity, 1969, p. 33.

[22]John 14:6; 3:16-18, 36 (New American Standard Bible)

[23]John 8:31, 32.

[24]John 16:13.

[25]Hammes, John A. *Humanistic Psychology: A Christian Interpretation.* New York: Grune & Stratton, 1971, p. 157.

[26]Lewis, C. S. *The Screwtape Letters.* London: Fontana Books, 1942, p. 9.

[27]1 Peter 5:8, 9; James 4:7, 8; John 8:44.

[28]Many Christians believe that the biblical account is essentially without error. A defense of the doctrine of inerrancy is beyond the scope of this book, but it is discussed in depth by Pinnock, C. H., *Biblical Revelation, op. cit.,* and by Young, Edward J., "Are the Scriptures Inerrant?" (in Tenney, *op. cit.,* pp. 103-119). See also *The Infallible Word: A Symposium by Members of the Faculty of Westminster Theological Seminary,* Philadelphia: Presbyterian and Reformed, 1946, and Lindsell, H., *The Battle for the Bible,* Grand Rapids: Zondervan, 1976.

[29]Carnell, *op. cit.,* p. 242.

Chapter Eight

PSYCHOLOGY ON A NEW FOUNDATION

BOOKS on the history of psychology often point out that psychology had its beginning in philosophy and theology. Only after the passing of many years and the diligent efforts of many people was psychology able to extricate itself from its historical roots and to assert its independence as a separate discipline. Any proposal that we should return to theology, therefore, is likely to be greeted with suspicion, if not outright condemnation. Why should a scientific psychologist be interested in God's existence as the source of all truth? Why should we bring the Bible into this discussion, even if we grant that this ancient book is the major way in which God has revealed himself? Why couldn't we build psychology on Zen Buddhism or humanism or existentialism or some different system?

E. J. Carnell has pointed us in the direction of an answer:

> The enigmatic situation in the modern world is that the scientist rejects the Christian world-view because it involves certain nonempirical, metaphysical hypotheses, while assuming for himself a truckload, each of which goes as much beyond sensory observation as does the Christian's postulate of the God Who has revealed Himself in Scripture. The Christian questions the sport of this game. Fair rules in the contest of hypothesis-making ought to dictate that the winner be he who can produce the best set of assumptions to account for the totality of reality....

> The Christian finds his system of philosophy in the Bible, to be sure, but he accepts this, not simply because it is in the Bible, but because, when tested, it makes better sense out of life than any other systems of philosophy make.[1]

The Christian doesn't maintain that his system has all the answers. He doesn't pretend that his position is logically

138   "air-tight," nor does he claim that he can give completely
conclusive proof of the Christian view. What he *does*
assert is that the biblical position is supported by a
considerable body of evidence, and that no other world
view is as logical, internally consistent, or able to give
meaning to the universe.

We now find ourselves in the area of *apologetics,* the
field of study concerned with defending the truthfulness
of the Christian religion. Whole textbooks have been
written on this subject,[2] so it would lead us too far afield
to enter into details of apologetics here. It is important,
however, that we briefly consider some of the data that
have been put forward to support the superiority of the
biblical system.

To begin, there is *evidence from personal experience.*
Many religious people, Christian and non-Christian,
have sought to base the truth of their religion on
subjective inner feelings. "I'm sure my religion must be
true," they assert, "because of the wonderful way in which
it has influenced my inner life."

There was a time, only a few years ago, when such
appeals to subjective validation would have been
immediately rejected, especially by psychologists.
Abnormal psychology and psychiatry books are filled
with cases of paranoid people who have built their lives
on an illusion, failing to realize that what one feels
subjectively is not always a reliable indicator of what exists
objectively. Psychologists have been quick to realize
that any feeling that has no basis in fact is mysticism and
can never prove anything—except perhaps that an
individual is having an experience.

As we have mentioned in earlier chapters, however,
subjectivism has recently become popular in Western
society. We appear to be moving into an "age of
unreason,"[3] where rational arguments are less important
than they once were, where one person's experience is
assumed to be as valid a guide to "truth" as the
experience of another, and where moral standards are
determined by the subjective maxim: "If it feels good, do

it!'' Even some theologians are concluding that it doesn't matter so much if religion is "true" as long as it arouses good feelings. Thus everyone can develop his own personal creed without worrying about such things as obedience to God or the validity of troublesome issues like the virgin birth, hell, the existence of miracles, or the resurrection of Christ. What one believes is of no great importance so long as you "have faith" in something.

The Christian acknowledges that experience is an important part of his religion. Feelings of joy, inner peace, hope, and love often accompany commitment to Christ; but emotions, important though they are, can never give, on their own, a verification for any system of belief. To escape from reason is to stampede toward skepticism, uncertainty, and sometimes despair. If the only standard of truth is my changing personal experience, then there can be no stability to my beliefs (since what I believe can change with my emotions). There can be no enduring ethical standards or basis for social justice (since each individual relies on his own transitory feelings about what is right and wrong and acts accordingly). There is no way to validate one's belief (since subjective experiences are difficult to verbalize and impossible to check against those of others in a scientific manner). There can be no basis for calling another person wrong (since his or her experience may be as "right" as mine). There can be no real hope for the future (since all I have to build on are the musings of my own mind). There can be no protection against individual fanaticism, dogmatism, and autosuggestion. To say "I feel that God exists" is no guarantee that he does exist. Subjective experience is important in our lives, and the Christian believes that there is an emotional aspect to Christianity. But if our beliefs are built on or validated by subjective experience alone, these beliefs will likely be vague, unstable, and ultimately inadequate.

If experience alone provides at best a weak justification for any system of beliefs, then perhaps we should turn to *arguments from logic*. If it could be shown that

140   Christianity or any other system is perfectly logical and
that its conclusions are deducible from reason alone, then
perhaps we would have a more solid basis for our
beliefs.

The Bible places great emphasis on the importance of
knowledge, wisdom, and use of the mind.[4] Men and
women are described as thinking beings whose most
complete understanding of God comes through what has
been divinely communicated in words. The Christian
who builds his faith on the Bible has no justification for
closing his mind and refusing to think. On the contrary,
he has both the freedom and encouragement to examine
his Christian beliefs intellectually, to determine as best
he can whether the biblical record is internally consistent
and logically viable.

In spite of this approval of rational thought, however,
the Christian does not claim that his system can be
deduced by reason alone. In the words of one philosopher,
"formal logic has limited power; it can neither establish
the truth of the premises a deduction uses, nor wholly
avoid the subjectivity of the philosopher, nor prove the
logical necessity of free actions and unique events. Its
primary value is as a negative criterion in exposing
inconsistencies and fallacies, and positively in helping us
see things as an ordered whole."[5]

The following syllogism is an example of logic not
leading to truth: All pigeons are monkeys; all
psychology professors are pigeons; therefore all
psychology professors are monkeys. According to
Carnell, this is a valid syllogism; it doesn't violate any
logical rules. Nevertheless, the conclusion is false
because the syllogism begins with two false premises. All
pigeons are not monkeys and all psychology professors
are not pigeons.[6] Logic is very important in philosophy,
psychology, and theology, but rational deduction by
itself can never be the basis on which we accept biblical
Christianity or any other position that might be proposed
as a new foundation for psychology. If we begin with faulty

141

assumptions we are unlikely ever to arrive at truth through logic alone.

In spite of their limitations, subjective personal experience and rational logic can both be means by which human beings know the truth, if these means are supplemented by *evidence from empirical facts.* As every psychologist knows, such facts come from careful observation of the universe and verification of these observations by others. Because the empiricist focuses his attention on events or observables in the environment, he is involved in something more than strict logical deduction, and since he makes his observations carefully, checking them against the findings of others, he has moved beyond subjective personal experience.

Like subjectivism and rationalism, empiricism also has problems. As we have seen in earlier chapters, the observer's presuppositions influence what he observes and sometimes even affect the data significantly. Complete objectivity is impossible. Further, the facts of science or history do not automatically lead us to the truth of any one world view. We may observe, for example, that the world is orderly but from this it does not necessarily follow that a God exists who created the order. Scientists can observe, summarize, and describe, but they go beyond empirical science when they begin to explain and interpret.

Why then do we elevate empirical facts to a high level of importance? The answer is that any world view, Christian or otherwise, must be consistent with the facts if it is to be taken seriously. In a court of law, the judge and jury seek to base their conclusions on facts. The greater the number of facts and the greater their internal consistency or agreement with each other, the more likely does one have the truth. The same applies when we come to evaluate a world view. It must be able to encompass all relevant data without forcing them to fit a preconceived system. We realize that any observation or interpretation of facts will be subject to personal bias, and we know that no world view can be proven with

142   anything like 100 percent certainty. Our task, therefore, is to accept the system which, while logically self-consistent and subjectively convincing, is best supported by the currently available data. As the supporting facts increase, so does our confidence in the validity of the supported system. Christians believe that the facts show their system to be superior to all others.

Christianity is a historical religion resting its case on an event in history that occurred many years ago: the resurrection of Jesus Christ. At the end of the last century an Oxford professor wrote that in his opinion it was "absurd to subordinate philosophy to certain historical events in Palestine—more and more absurd."[7] Many modern psychologists and psychology students might agree, especially when it is proposed that the truth of the resurrection is of great importance to twentieth-century science. But this alleged absurdity is the basis on which the Christian system is built. As one of the biblical writers stated, the Christian position is worthless unless Christ did in fact rise from the dead.[8]

It is not unusual for psychologists or psychiatrists to apply their scientific skills to the study of history. Freud, Erikson, and Fromm, for example, wrote not only about history but about historical religious figures as well.[9] The historian's methods must differ from those of the behaviorist or experimental psychologist who studies ongoing repeatable events, but the study of history can nevertheless be scientific. "If we mean by 'science' the attempt to find out what really happens," one author has written, "then history is science. It demands the same kind of dedication, the same ruthlessness, the same passion for exactness, as physics"[10] or (we might add) "as scientific psychology."

There is abundant historical evidence to show that Christ actually did rise from the dead.[11] Many people inspected the empty tomb, for example, over 500 people saw Jesus himself at different times after Easter, and subsequently nobody was able to find his body—which

143 would have stopped rumors of the resurrection. A lot of first-century people didn't like the story of Christ's having risen, yet we have no evidence that anybody was able to disprove it. It could be argued, of course, that the resurrection was a hoax, but it seems highly unlikely that a sad and defeated little band of cowardly disciples could have planned a logic-tight story powerful enough to turn them and others into irresistible missionaries who proclaimed their beliefs in spite of persecution and who willingly faced martyrdom. Surely someone would have told the truth eventually and produced a corpse if the resurrection story was really a cover-up.

At this point the reader might protest that the evidence is based on the writings of New Testament writers whose reports are biased and of questionable accuracy. Of course they were biased—but so, as we have seen, is the work of every other observer. At least the biblical writers were honest enough to describe the faults of early Christian leaders as well as their strengths. Such balanced character studies are an argument in favor of the Bible's historical authenticity. Thus, to declare a priori that the biblical data are inaccurate may be more a reflection of anti-Christian prejudice than of factual knowledge. The New Testament message is found in roughly 4,000 Greek manuscripts (some of which date back to A.D. 150 and earlier), 13,000 manuscripts of isolated portions, and 8,000 Latin manuscripts. Apart from some minor discrepancies over details, these documents agree in their accounts of Christ's life events. Extrabiblical corroboration is found in the writings of Josephus and other early historians.[12]

Critics have asserted that the resurrection account is a figment of somebody's imagination, the result of mass hallucinations (whatever they are), or the outworkings of some "Passover plot." Maybe Jesus never died at all, it has been suggested, but simply went into an unconscious swoon on the cross. In the cool of the tomb he recovered enough to shake off the grave clothes, roll back the massive stone traditionally used to seal tombs in Jesus' culture, overcome the tough Roman guard, and appear

144

looking hale and hearty before his followers. Others have suggested that in some way the body stayed dead (and hidden from skeptics who wanted to disprove the resurrection), but that the "psychological parts" of Jesus rose and brought about a "spiritual resurrection." All of these are highly speculative hypotheses for which there is not one solid piece of historical evidence.

But then comes the critic's strongest challenge. "The resurrection could not have happened because it is a violation of the laws of nature. Men who are dead don't come alive again." Laws of nature, however, are only descriptions of what has happened in the past and predictions of what will probably occur in the future. There is no irrefutable evidence for the external existence of "natural laws" and they certainly cannot be used to tell us what *cannot* happen. Thus, the investigator should

> ...first consult history, and after deciding by historical evidence what has happened, should then choose his laws within the limits of historical actuality. The non-Christian thinker, intent on repudiating miracles, proceeds by a reverse method. He chooses his law without regard to historical limits, and then tries to rewrite history to fit his law. But surely this method is not only the reverse of the Christian method, it is clearly the reverse of rational procedure as well.[13]

In all of ancient history, few events can be better supported than the resurrection of Jesus Christ. Of all the attempts to understand Christ's last days, the resurrection account fits the data better than any other explanation. Of all events in history, however, there is no event that men are less inclined to believe. If it can be shown that the resurrection did not occur, then we have good reason for rejecting much of Christianity. Jesus predicted that he would rise again, and the Bible repeatedly proclaims that the resurrection did in fact occur. If it did not occur, then at least a part of the Bible

145

is a fraud or at best the conclusions of deluded simpletons. If the Bible is wrong about the resurrection, then we can legitimately conclude that it might also be wrong about such things as Christ's claims to be God's son or his call for individuals to obey and commit their lives to him.[14] If, however, we acknowledge the validity of the resurrection, we are virtually forced to admit the reality and power of a superhuman God and we must give serious consideration to his claims on our lives. To avoid this, many people prefer to find some way to explain away the resurrection—even if it takes more faith to believe in the explanation than in the reality of the resurrection event itself.

In this discussion we have said nothing about the impressive body of archaeological and historical evidence supporting the biblical message. Nelson Glueck, a non-Christian archaeologist who spent much of his life studying biblical archaeology, reached the conclusion that no archaeological discovery contradicts or disputes the historical statements of the Bible. On the contrary, as archaeological evidence accumulates it appears to give more and more support to the accuracy of the biblical records.[15]

Since Christianity is a religion based on historical events, it seems wise that it be verified with historical and archaeological evidence. For the psychologist who is not much interested in history, however, this may raise some problems. Why, it might be asked, don't we use psychological facts to verify the Christian position?

In the first place, there are not that many known psychological facts about religion. Psychologists and others have studied such issues as conversion, moral development, or religious experience, but on the whole the psychology of religion is a relatively new (though growing) field. Even if we did have more psychological facts about religious behavior, we would still be faced with a limitation that archaeologists and historians must also acknowledge: although there is impressive empirical and other evidence to support the claims of Christianity,

146   an individual's religious beliefs, like one's philosophical
presuppositions, can never be conclusively proven by
science. It seems logical that we should put our confidence
in the system or person whose claims are best supported
by the available data—which gets us to the issue of faith.
Faith, as we have said earlier, is not a blind leap into the
unknown; it is the putting of one's trust and dependence on
something which evidence shows to be trustworthy. The
Christian puts his trust in the Christ who is revealed in the
Bible; the non-Christian puts his trust in science, man,
philosophy or a number of other non-theistic alternatives.

This brings us back, full circle, to the five basic
presuppositions (empiricism, determinism, relativism,
reductionism, and naturalism) on which psychology has
thus far been built. To be a psychologist, one must take a
position concerning each of these operational
assumptions. Many psychologists appear to accept them
without giving them much thought. If we are to build
psychology on the one major assumption that God exists
and is the source of all truth, however, the original
assumptions will have to be altered to make them
consistent with the new premise.

As described in chapter 5, empiricism maintains that
the only reliable knowledge comes through the senses
and is discoverable by controlled experiments or other
objective observations. In place of this, we propose an
expanded empiricism which assumes that sense
experience is one channel, but only one of several
channels, through which truth comes to man from God.
Expanded empiricism permits us to maintain a belief in the
value of empirical studies of human (and animal)
behavior. They are one productive way by which we gain
factual knowledge and access to the truth. But
empiricism can never be the only way to learn about man
nor can it give a complete picture of man. The human
being is a complex individual who must be studied in a
variety of ways, including, but not limited to, analysis of
overt observable behavior. Unlike humanism, which tries to

147 study the whole of man but rejects the existence or influence of divinity, expanded empiricism acknowledges that God exists and can have a direct effect as influential on man as the effects of emotions, intellect, past experience, innate potentialities, or reinforcement contingencies.

Expanded empiricism does not object if a researcher decides at times to define concepts operationally. One must not go further, however, and assume that an operational definition is an all-inclusive description of the truth or that nonoperational definitions are inaccurate and useless. Likewise, quantitative measurements should remain an important part of psychology, but one must resist thinking that everything worth studying may be described mathematically. In all of our attempts to discover the truth, complete objectivity is desirable but unattainable. The psychologist, therefore, must go on collecting empirical data with as much objectivity as he can muster, but he must recognize that his data are likely to be biased. They must be tested against other scientific data and against evidence that comes from such sources as logical deduction, intuition, and special revelation as found in the Bible.

Turning to the topic of determinism, we encounter an issue that is not only a rock-bottom assumption in psychology, but one that has long interested theologians as well. The problem for both psychology and theology is the extent to which behavior is determined. The followers of Freud, Skinner, and John Calvin would agree that all behavior is completely determined, although the Freudians and Skinnerians propose nontheistic "natural" causes in contrast with the Calvinist's belief that a sovereign God determines everything. Such denial of human freedom contradicts our own personal experience and seems to go against both biblical and nonbiblical views about the existence of free will. Perhaps for the present we can make a place for both hypotheses—*determinism and free will*— even though this view will be challenged both by strict determinists and by nondeterminists.

Let us assume that a high school graduate finds himself in a situation where he must choose between a number of alternatives for the future. Perhaps he is deciding whether to attend university, enlist in the navy, enter his father's business, join a commune, accept a job in the community, or spend a year thumbing his way around the world. We can assume that he is free to choose between these alternatives, but it does not necessarily follow that he is equally disposed to each of these possibilities. His genetic endowment, past experiences, unconscious fears, future expectations, social pressures—like his girlfriend's desire to get married—and even direct supernatural influences may all have a bearing on his choice, thus making some alternatives much more likely than others. He may, in the end, decide "by his own free will" to join the navy. Yet his decision was in large measure limited or determined by influences in his past and present life.

The debate over determinism is still a live issue in psychology and in theology.[16] Although it seems unlikely that behavior is completely determined, especially if individuals are to be held responsible for their actions, the issue is by no means settled. A psychology built on the premise of God's existence as the source of truth does not rule out determinism *or* free will. There can be place for both. This new foundation for psychology does maintain, however, that to the list of determinants of behavior we must add the direct influence of the supernatural. God does influence us through the power of his Holy Spirit. The devil and his angels are also active and influential. To overlook such nonhuman forces is to eliminate some potent and relevant determinants of human behavior.

The proposed new foundation of psychology lets us accept belief in expanded empiricism and in both free will and determinism, but the assumption of unlimited relativism is more difficult to retain. If there is no absolute truth, no absolute standard of right and wrong, no absolute measure of good and bad, then we are in danger

149 of plunging ultimately into confusion and anarchy. At the other extreme, assumption of unlimited absolutism also raises problems. For something to be absolute it must be independent of time (eternally true), unchanging (immutably true), independent of space (universally true), and apart from man (discoverable but not created by human beings).[17] Based on his reading of the Bible, the Christian believes that God himself fits these criteria and that in him there is absolute truth, goodness, perfection, power, justice, mercy, sovereignty, wisdom, and love.

The problem for men and women comes in grasping what is absolute. Although absolute truth never changes, our perception, understanding, and interpretation of absolute truth does change. The new foundation for psychology, therefore, leads to what we might call *biblical absolutism:* the view that the individual should search the Bible for absolutes, or for general principles that can guide and increase our understanding of behavior. In those situations where the Bible is silent, we try to establish our values and ethical decisions as much as possible in accordance with the spirit of biblical principles.

Belief in biblically-based absolutes does not mean that we must jettison pragmatism as a guide to truth. That something works may be one indication of truth even though it cannot be the final criterion. We must realize that what works for one person may not work for another, and that some things (a "successful" career as a thief or prostitute, for example) may work, but working does not make them right. Superstitious acts like carrying a rabbit's foot may seem to work in bringing good luck, but the desirable events of one's life may have nothing to do with the influence of a lucky charm. Pragmatism, therefore, may point to the truth of an idea but in addition we must test our conclusions against the Bible and against other facts that have come through the findings of science or the humanities.

Even with impressive supporting data, we cannot be 100 percent certain about our scientific conclusions. Only

150

an omniscient God has certain knowledge; man, at least while he lives on earth, usually must be content with probabilities. We must remember, however, that all things are not equally probable. The data we accumulate in our studies can help us decide which of several alternatives is more probably true. It is here that knowledge of the Bible can also be helpful, giving insight into the unchanging truth that God has chosen to reveal in his written Word.

Turning to the issue of reductionism, the view that behavior can be reduced to smaller units that are easier to study, we find that it must be considerably modified if it is to be maintained as a part of the new foundation for psychology. It is certainly convenient to break our subject matter into smaller units more accessible to precise investigation. In doing so, however, we must not assume that analysis of the parts necessarily leads to greater understanding of the whole human being. We cannot even assume that all psychological processes can be broken into smaller pieces. It may be that concepts like love, hope, personality, cognition, or religious experience, for example, cannot be divided into analyzable parts.

Our new foundation for psychology, therefore, leads us to a *modified reductionism:* an acknowledgment that only some of the subject matter of psychology may be divisible into smaller units of analysis. The task of psychological research is not to fragment human behavior, but to study man in his wholeness and with as much precision as possible; we must deliberately test our findings against the truths of special revelation and the findings of researchers in other disciplines and other branches of psychology. "Nothing buttery" must be abandoned. For example, human sexual behavior may, for purposes of study, be reduced to an analysis of physiological drives, but it does not follow that sex is nothing but biology.

To this point we have altered the established presuppositions of psychology and suggested that they be retained in a modified form. When we come to the

151 assumption of naturalism, such an alteration is not possible. Instead, nontheistic naturalism must be rejected as diametrically opposite to the theistic presupposition lying at the base of our new foundation. In place of naturalism we propose *Christian supernaturalism*. Such a view does not deny that the world is orderly, that there may be laws of behavior, or that we should seek for natural explanations. It does maintain that all order originates with a sovereign God who created the universe and holds it all together.[18] Human beings are *not* alone in a universe indifferent to their fate. There *is* a power transcending them which is concerned about them and able to influence their destiny.

This leads us to propose one additional working assumption for psychology: a *biblical anthropology*. By "anthropology" here we are not referring to the social science of ethnic groups and primitive societies. Rather we refer to a view of man, and we are proposing that psychology should accept a model of man derived from the Bible.

The Bible presents a holistic approach to human beings. Behaviorists have tended to view man as a physical organism who responds to environmental stimulation but has little freedom, dignity, or self-determination. Other psychologists, including the humanists, while not denying man's physical nature, have proposed that he is more: a thinking, emotional, social creature, for example. Biblical anthropology goes even further. Man is physical, rational, emotional, and social—but he is also spiritual, a being who was created in the divine image and given a special place in the universe.

Regretfully, man deliberately rebelled against God and refused to obey him. For this action, God justly condemned the human race. But God is also found to be merciful and loving. He has provided a way (through confession of sin and belief in Jesus Christ, God's Son) by which individuals can be forgiven for their sin and restored to fellowship with God. In themselves, men and

152

women are not innately good or always improving, but neither are they morally neutral. They are innately sinful, a fact that our declining morals and breakdown of law and order are serving to confirm. There need not be despair about this, however, since God has shown himself to be in ultimate control of the universe. He will guarantee a bright and everlasting future for those who commit their lives to him.[19] These conclusions could never be discovered empirically or rationally. They are revealed to individuals who can either accept or reject them. Surely, however, they are as consistent with the facts at our disposal as the conclusion either that man is a mere machine or that he is an animal of some sort which every day in every way is getting better and better.[20]

Our proposed new foundation for psychology is now complete. As shown in Figure 2, it rests on one basic premise, a corollary, and six working assumptions, all of which derive from the one premise which forms the basis for a new approach to psychology.

Figure 2:
The New Foundation for Psychology
The proposed new system rests on one major premise from which there is derived a corollary and six working assumptions, all of which are consistent with and supported by the underlying premise.

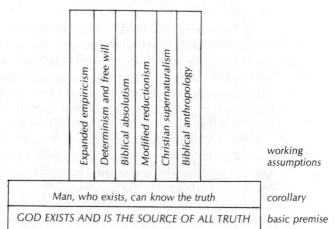

| Expanded empiricism | Determinism and free will | Biblical absolutism | Modified reductionism | Christian supernaturalism | Biblical anthropology | working assumptions |

Man, who exists, can know the truth | corollary

GOD EXISTS AND IS THE SOURCE OF ALL TRUTH | basic premise

153

Footnotes
Chapter 8

[1] Carnell, Edward J. *An Introduction to Christian Apologetics*. Grand Rapids: Eerdmans, 1948, pp. 94, 102.

[2] See, for example, Carnell, *op. cit.;* Pinnock, Clark H., *Set Forth Your Case*, Chicago: Moody, 1967; Ramm, Bernard, *Protestant Christian Evidences*, Chicago: Moody, 1953; *Varieties of Christian Apologetics*, Grand Rapids: Baker, 1961; Montgomery, John Warwick (ed.), *Christianity for the Tough-Minded*, Minneapolis: Bethany, 1973.

[3] Maddocks, Melvin. "The New Cult of Madness: Thinking as a Bad Habit," *Time*, March 13, 1972, pp. 27, 30.

[4] See, for example, Stott, John R. W., *Your Mind Matters*, Downers Grove, Illinois: Inter-Varsity, 1973.

[5] Holmes, Arthur F. *Faith Seeks Understanding*. Grand Rapids: Eerdmans, 1971, pp. 51-2. In his book, Holmes has clearly shown both the limits and the power of logic. "Religious belief," he writes in another context, "is neither incompatible with rational cogency nor as accessible to reason as the conclusion of a mathematical proof. It stands in between" (p. 58).

[6] Carnell, *op. cit.*, p. 59.

[7] MacKinnon, D. M., *et al. Objections to Christian Belief*. Baltimore: Penguin, 1963, p. 51.

[8] 1 Corinthians 15:14-17.

[9] Freud, Sigmund, *Totem and Taboo* (1913), London: Routledge and Kegan Paul, 1950; *Moses and Monotheism* (1939), London: Hogarth Press, 1964; Erikson, Erik H., *Young Man Luther: A Study of Psychoanalysis and History*, New York: Norton, 1958; Fromm, Erich, *You Shall Be As Gods: A Radical Interpretation of the Old Testament and Its Tradition*. See also Schweitzer, Albert, *The Psychiatric Study of Jesus*, Boston: The Beacon Press, 1948.

[10] From J. A. Passmore, "The Objectivity of History," quoted by Montgomery, John W., "The Relevance of Scripture Today," in Tenney, Merrill C. (ed.), *The Bible: The Living Word of Revelation*, Grand Rapids: Zondervan, 1968, p. 209.

[11] Some of this is summarized by Anderson, J. N. D., *The Evidence for the Resurrection*, London: Inter-Varsity, 1950; Tenney, Merrill C., *The Reality of the Resurrection*, New York: Harper & Row, 1963; Ramm, Bernard, *Protestant Christian Evidences, op. cit.;* and Morrison, F., *Who Moved the Stone?* London: Faber & Faber, 1958.

[12] Pinnock, C. H. *Set Forth Your Case, op. cit.* (See especially chapters 9-11); Bruce, F. F. *The New Testament Documents: Are They Reliable?* Grand Rapids: Eerdmans, 1943.

[13] Clark, G. H. "Miracles: History and Natural Law," *The Evangelical Quarterly* **12**, 1940, p. 34, quoted in Carnell, *op. cit.*, p. 258.

[14] John 14:23; 1 John 2:15-17. See also 1 Corinthians 15:12-16.

[15] Bruce, F. F., *op. cit.;* Keller, Werner, *The Bible as History*, New York: William Morrow, 1956. The conclusion of Glueck is cited in a section on archaeology in Harrison, R. K., *Introduction to the Old Testament*, Grand Rapids: Eerdmans, 1969, p. 94.

[16] See, for example, Leona Tyler's presidential address to the American Psychological Association: Tyler, Leona E. "Design for a Hopeful Psychology," *American Psychologist* **28**, 1973, pp. 1021-9.

[17] Hammes, John A. *Humanistic Psychology: A Christian Interpretation*. New York: Grune and Stratton, 1971, p. 25.

154

[18]Hebrews 1:1-3; Colossians 1:16, 17.

[19]These biblical views of man are discussed more fully in the author's book, *Search for Reality: Psychology and the Christian* (Collins, Gary R., Santa Ana, California: Vision House, 1969, pp. 20-32.) Among the Bible verses that give support to these conclusions are Genesis 1:27; Romans 3:23, 10:9, 6:23; and 1 John 1:8, 9. See also Berkouwer, G. C., *Man: The Image of God,* Grand Rapids: Eerdmans, 1962.

[20]In commenting on a rough draft of this manuscript, one of the reviewers commented at this point: "It is man's current abnormality which gets naturalistic psychologists into trouble. For, like all naturalists, the psychologist looks at the current state of man and says that that is how man essentially is, whereas the Christian says that the current state of man is abnormal. One is never able to have a good anthropology or psychology or anything else unless he recognizes that (1) the current state of man is an abnormal one and (2) our knowledge about what man essentially is cannot be gained completely from empirical data (because what stands in front of man is not what man essentially is, but what he has made himself to be through the fall) nor from rational data (because the investigator himself is fallen and is therefore unable to reason with complete accuracy). In other words, both the observer and the subject observed are abnormal. For this reason, revelation is necessary."

Chapter Nine

PSYCHOLOGY

IN THE FUTURE

WHEN a medical doctor is consulted about an illness, he usually considers the symptoms, does a physical examination, makes some kind of diagnosis, and then initiates a series of treatments which he hopes will make the patient better. We have attempted to do something similar in the preceding pages. We have looked at psychology, considered its history, examined its healthy and unhealthy characteristics, offered the diagnosis that psychology suffers from "inadequate presuppositions," and prescribed some surgery to change the assumptions on which our science rests. It is quite possible that the patient won't want to undergo the surgery, but we are proposing what we think will have to be done about psychology's current problems to assure a good prognosis for the future.

Of course many psychologists already are working to improve their discipline and are attempting to move it toward a healthier future. A recent symposium led to the sobering conclusion that ours is

> ...a psychology whose metaphysical framework or foundation is outdated, based on a philosophy of science discarded decades ago by physics (long the model for psychology). Not only is this foundation obsolete, but the conception of its subject matter, man, is no longer appropriate if indeed it ever was. We have findings that are irrelevant and meaningless to man, based on experiments that study nonrepresentative, atypical samples of subjects who don't believe what we tell them and who respond in terms of their own perception of what the experimental situation is all about. Our data are often analyzed and interpreted incorrectly, and conclusions drawn without legitimate substantiation. Psychology lacks relevance and scientific and philosophical sophistication, conducts trivial and technically incorrect experiments, and presents a demeaning and defeating image of man.

158
> The portrait is not excessively overdrawn, depressing though it may be, for each of the charges has a firm basis in reality...[1]

In psychology we are much better at naming, describing, and diagnosing our difficulties than we are at curing them. Too often, we give vivid portrayals of our problems, but follow these with weak and vague proposals for the future. "Psychology's only hope is science!"[2] writes one author, while others talk about being "more flexible," "changing our emphasis," "becoming more concerned about humans," "expanding psychology's narrow definition," and a host of other remedies that say nothing very practical about how we proceed to make psychology more effective in the future.

No one person is likely to come up with a perfectly workable prescription for progress in psychology, but we can begin to resolve our difficulties if psychologists and psychology students together start asking ourselves (and each other) such questions as the following:

> What are *my* underlying assumptions about man and about psychology?

> How do these affect my behavior and influence my psychological work?

> What assumptions would be better (more logical, more consistent with current knowledge, more comprehensive, freer of inner contradictions, etc.)?

> Is my work in psychology of any relevance or significance?

> Am I guilty of contributing to the problems in psychology (described in the quotation on the previous page)?

> How can I change to make my work more effective?

159   Continual self-evaluation, accompanied by sincere attempts to change, can be a first step pointing psychology in a new direction. It is the thesis of this book, however, that self-evaluation and creative innovation are not enough. Psychology will continue to be incomplete and weakened as long as it persists in denying God and ignoring the biblical revelation. Instead, psychology must be built on a foundation that acknowledges the existence of God as a supreme Being who is the source of all truth. There are, however, a number of difficulties with this proposal, difficulties that must at least be acknowledged even if they cannot for the moment be resolved.

First, the proposed new foundation is largely built on ideas that come from a controversial book, the Bible. Why should any thinking psychologist seek to build a modern science on the authority of an ancient book, written in a prescientific era and filled with apparent errors and inconsistencies? To answer, we might begin by noting that the errors, inconsistencies, and contradictions are not nearly so plentiful as critics believe. In 1800 the French Institute in Paris issued a list of eighty-two errors in the Bible which they believed would decisively destroy Christianity. Today, less than 200 years later, not one of these so-called errors remains.[3] Archaeological, historical, and linguistic studies have shown that biblical inconsistencies are far fewer than might have been thought in the past. And even if minor contradictions and apparent errors do remain, this in itself is no reason for throwing out the Bible. Every system contains at least some uncertainties and intellectual difficulties.[4] The rational person tries to find the system with the fewest problems. The psychologist may not like the idea that God exists or that he has revealed truth through the Bible, but this view should at least be seriously considered before it is replaced by some other system that is less coherent, internally consistent, comprehensive, supported by external data, or able to explain the behavior of man and his universe.

160

A second objection to the new foundation is that it is too confining. How can we have free and open investigation when we are bound by the restraints of a system of theology? There are two responses to this question. First, no investigator is completely free of presuppositional constraints. As we have shown, everyone is guided by some belief system, theistic or otherwise. What we are proposing is not necessarily any more confining (and because of its breadth is probably less confining) than the nontheistic framework within which psychology works at present.

Second, the proposed foundation still leaves room for a variety of viewpoints. Just as there can be different clinical viewpoints or systems of experimental psychology, so there can be different Christian theologies all based on the same initial premise. The Bible is the Christian's guidebook, but no one individual or group is likely to have a corner on all truth. We are finite, imperfect creatures, whose interpretations are sometimes wrong. So we continue to study the Bible, searching for a clearer view of the written truth, just as we explore the universe scientifically in order better to understand the truths found in nature. The longer one's list of prior assumptions the more one is bound by them, but the person who accepts a long list of presuppositions without even thinking much about them is the most confined of all.

A third and perhaps stronger objection to the new foundation is that it seems to represent regression rather than progress; a step backward rather than a thrust ahead. Freud, Darwin, Bertrand Russell, and a host of others rejoiced as they watched science move away from religious "superstitions" of the past. Surely, then, a return to theism could not possibly be interpreted as a progressive move. Perhaps we should just keep moving along as we have in the past, convinced that "psychology's only hope is science!"

When we consider how hard some psychologists have fought (and are still fighting) to establish their discipline as

161   a science, we can understand their reluctance to make any moves toward theology, philosophy, or the humanities. In universities and colleges around the world, students are trained to think of psychology as a science, any suggestions to the contrary being met with the strongest opposition. It is likely, therefore, that proposals such as we have put forth in this book will at different times be ignored, criticized, or resisted. The only alternative to scientific naturalism is ultimately some kind of supernaturalism, and in the minds of many psychologists, belief in the supernatural is the antithesis of science. Evidently in psychology many would rather cling to a limiting methodology and a set of presuppositions derived from physics than admit that truth might also be discovered through some nonscientific means. But in spite of opinions to the contrary, a return to the Bible is not necessarily a return to immature and superstitious religion. Neither is it a forsaking of science. It is, instead, a broadening of our approach so that we are exposed to fresh new evidence and enabled to extend the scope of our investigations about man far beyond their present constricted empirical boundaries.

Important as they are, these objections to the new foundation for psychology are secondary to two further issues not yet discussed. First is the question of whether the new foundation is really something different. Is it a stimulus for a truly new and better psychology, or is it a watering down of science, a not-too-subtle attempt to reintroduce religion into psychology, a restatement of what most Christians in psychology have always done, or a proposal to eliminate psychology altogether, replacing it with a Christianity clothed in psychological jargon? The second major question concerns the feasibility of the new psychology. Will it really work and, if so, how? These questions are of such importance that in one way or another the remainder of this book will be an attempt to answer them.

162   Let us begin with a consideration of whether psychology
built on a biblical foundation would in fact be
something unique. Since psychology usually is defined as
the study of human behavior, it is natural that we should
begin first with the questions of who man is and what is his
place in the universe.

Stated concisely, the Bible declares that God is both the
Creator and Sustainer of the entire universe, including
the earth and its people. Through his Son Jesus Christ, God
brought all things into being and it is currently by his
power that all things are being held together.[5] God is not a
"prime mover" who got the universe going and then left
it on its own; he is active in the universe today, still very
much aware of and in control of his divine creation.
There is, of course, considerable debate concerning the
exact manner in which God brought his creation into
existence. The Bible is clear in stating, however, that men
and women were created as beings who are unique and
of special value to God. Mankind was formed in the
image of God (and not vice versa as some psychologists
have asserted).

Unlike animals which are guided by instinct or robots
which are wound up and programmed to act in specified
ways, human beings were given moral discernment (to
tell right from wrong), responsibility for their actions, and
so much freedom that they could even rebel against the
Creator. Man did rebel and by this action condemned
himself, (since under God's system of perfect justice
rebellion always must be punished fairly). The same God
who is just and holy, however, has also revealed himself
as being merciful and loving. Not willing that any should
perish, he sent his sinless Son into the world to pay for
the sins of mankind and to make the way possible for
individuals who so desire to come back into
communion with God. Man still retains his freedom and
can choose either to come back to God or to keep on
rebelling. Some find their way back through confession of
sin and acknowledgment of the Lordship of Jesus Christ;
others continue rebelling either by deliberate resistance

against God or by ignoring him.

Mankind, therefore, can be divided into two groups: the natural man who is still alienated from God and destined to spend eternity in a place of punishment, and the redeemed man who has returned to God, has been adopted back into his family and who has been promised an eternal life with God.

Even though mankind can in general be divided into these two groups it does not follow that individuals can be divided into parts. Humans can be studied from a physiological, psychological, social, or spiritual perspective but each person regardless of his or her relationship with God, is a holistic being who functions as a unit.

Many psychologists would accept a holistic definition of man but the theocentric approach to mankind and his universe is far removed from anything existing in mainstream psychology today. Some psychological systems think of man as only a complex machine; others see him as little more than an animal high on the evolutionary scale. Most psychologists view man as a free and morally discerning creature of chance origin who nevertheless is molded by his culture and moving toward an unknown, probably hopeless, destiny. No psychological system sees man as the creation of a supreme Being who oversees human behavior, has the power to intervene in individuals' lives, and who maintains responsibility for holding together the whole creation, including man and his environment.

The division of mankind into two categories, natural and redeemed, is even more divergent from the thinking of psychologists. In biological and much psychological functioning, both groups are the same, but the believer in Christ is, in addition, a new creature with potential for a more complete understanding of the universe, a new system of values, a more loving and peaceful life style, and a confident hope for the future.[6] Such a view of man and his universe would greatly influence our approach to counseling and the ways in which we attempt to

164   understand and study human behavior.

In their study of human behavior, some psychologists in the past have tended to utilize positivistic behavioristic methods which assume that when something cannot be observed, it cannot be studied and may not even exist. Thus, concepts like hope, will, intention, faith, or even experience were swept aside as being of no interest to scientific psychology. Within recent years, the winds of change have been blowing and psychologists have begun to acknowledge that man is more than his observable behavior. But it becomes very difficult to broaden our research techniques while we are still bound to the old presuppositions, especially those of empiricism and reductionism. Thus, research, especially experimental research, continues in a stereotyped format: review the literature on what has been done in the past; formulate a hypothesis for testing, usually expressed as a "null hypothesis"; plan the procedures (including practical decisions) about how to manipulate the independent variable, measure the dependent variable, and control other relevant variables; do the study; assemble, organize, and analyze the data, preferably using statistics; draw conclusions, being careful not to generalize too far beyond the data; and write the report, preferably in "APA style." This technique undoubtedly will continue to be used in the future as in the past. It is ideally suited for the narrow, behavioristic type of experiment that continues to be an important part of psychology.

For the broader study of behavior, however, we need a fresh approach to knowledge based on a new set of presuppositions. This approach must recognize

—that man is unique in the universe (not just an animal);

—that our object of study is a creature of worth, volition, and responsibility; and

—that an almighty and loving God has the power to intervene in individuals' lives.

165   Several years ago John R. Platt of the University of
Chicago published an interesting analysis of scientific
thinking.[7] Platt had noticed that some fields of science
seem to move ahead very rapidly, while others (probably
including psychology) limp along without making much
noticeable progress. The difference seemed to be that the
rapidly moving fields utilize a method that Platt has
called "strong inference." In this approach the investigator
begins by reviewing the literature and coming up with a
hypothesis. Then, before designing experiments to
support the hypothesis (or disprove the null hypothesis),
he writes down every conclusion he can think of that
would disprove the original hypothesis. This is
illustrated below:

ORIGINAL HYPOTHESIS
This hypothesis is invalid if: *–alternative a is true* *–alternative b is true* *–alternative c is true, etc.*

The next step is to think of a way in which we can
disprove each of the alternatives. If all of the alternatives
can be disproven or shown to be false, then the original
hypothesis is probably correct. If none or some of the
alternatives can be disproven, then the hypothesis is of
questionable validity. We must come up with a different
hypothesis and repeat the procedure. The hypothesis that is
most probably true is the one that best survives this
repeated analysis. Stated differently, the original
hypothesis is probably true if all of the alternatives are
shown to be false. By following this outline, Platt suggests,
we will start producing journal articles saying, "Here is
my conclusion. This conclusion would be invalid if (i),
(ii),...or (n) are true. We shall now describe experiments
to eliminate these alternatives." This procedure is widely
used in molecular biology and physics, where
researchers attempt to disprove each of the alternatives

with a concise and carefully executed scientific experiment. The most valid hypothesis is assumed to be the one that best survives after being subjected to a number of crucial tests.

This approach does not differ greatly from what psychologists are already doing. In the study of human behavior, however, we must recognize that while some of the "alternatives" in the diagram might be examined experimentally, other issues simply cannot be. By building psychology on this proposed new foundation we continue to use experimental techniques wherever we can, but we must also modify our methodology to make room for data derived from logical deduction, personal experience, and study of the Bible. In so doing we are able to investigate empirical as well as nonempirical (even religious) issues within a scientific framework.[8]

As a specific example, let us consider how our new foundation, coupled with Platt's proposal, could be used to investigate Freud's famous conclusion that religious believers are really neurotic.

HYPOTHESIS: *Religious people are neurotic*

This hypothesis is invalid if:
(a) *religious people are as mentally healthy as or healthier than nonbelievers*
(b) *only some religious people are neurotic; but others are not*
(c) *the Bible states that religious people cannot be neurotic*
(d) *the hypothesis is illogical*

Alternatives (a) and (b) could be disproven by the use of empirical data, while alternative (c) requires careful study of the Bible if it is to be disproven, and alternative (d) depends on logical analysis. If we were to write "true" or "false" next to each of the statements, we would put "false" next to alternative (d). There is nothing illogical about the hypothesis. Alternative (c) might also be marked "false" since the Bible does not specifically say anything about religion and neurosis (although it does *imply* that

167

belief contributes to mental health). Alternatives (a) and (b) cannot be marked "false" because they are supported by empirical evidence. Thus the hypothesis that religious belief causes neurosis is of questionable validity, and our task is to find other hypotheses (e.g., "religious belief protects us from neurosis," "neurotic people are always religious," "religion can have both a healthy and an unhealthy influence on believers," etc.) and start over again.

Such a procedure does not guarantee that we will be kept from error. In the social sciences it is difficult to design concise experiments to prove or disprove conclusively each of the alternatives in our diagram. It is also difficult to develop a complete set of alternatives, but by broadening our approach to include biblical, rational, and other nonexperimental data we can have more evidence for our conclusions and fewer restrictions on the scope of our investigations.

This approach, if applied consistently, would include empirical scientific methodology—but it does more. It takes psychology beyond empirical science and puts biblical exegesis and logical deduction on at least an equal plane with empiricism. To assume that God exists as the source of all truth is not to throw out the scientific method. The new psychology, like the old, seeks to attain as accurate an understanding of the natural world as possible. Although the new psychology makes full use of scientific techniques, striving to observe with precision and to draw conclusions with caution, it is not restricted by or limited to the empirical scientific method. If we believe that God reveals truths about the world through philosophical logic or through the humanities, for example, we should be free to make use of them. In addition, the teachings of the Bible must be thoroughly researched and applied to our study of the phenomenon under investigation. If a psychologist wants to understand, say, why some teen-age boy becomes delinquent, he will study the problem by the established methods of scientific psychology, but he will also search the Scriptures to determine what, if anything, the Bible says about the issue.

How does one search the Bible to ascertain with as much clarity as possible what God has revealed in it? This question brings us to *hermeneutics:* the science and art of interpreting the Bible. Currently within theology, hermeneutics and the issue of biblical inerrancy are among the most hotly debated subjects, but some principles of biblical interpretation appear to be emerging from the debate. To understand the Bible, for example, it is widely agreed that we should know something about the culture, history, and geography of the Middle Eastern world in which the biblical writers lived. It is also important to recognize the biblical use of metaphors, similes, and other figures of speech. In current speech, for example, we may say "It's raining cats and dogs," but nobody takes such expressions literally and neither should we do so with biblical figures of speech. Further, as with other writings, passages in the Bible should be viewed in context, not as isolated phrases or sentences.

A basic rule is that obscure passages in the Bible should always give way to clear passages. According to Ramm, "the theologian must basically rest his theology on those passages that are clear and not upon those that are obscure....Essential truth is not tucked away in some incidental remark in Scripture nor in some passage that remains ambiguous in its meaning even after being subjected to very thorough research."[9] Many faulty theological doctrines and erroneous doctrines and erroneous conclusions have been built from obscure passages of Scripture.

More controversial, perhaps, is the rule that the Bible should be interpreted literally. In common life, writers seldom expect readers to look into their works trying to find double meanings or private messages. Why, then, do people read the Bible as if it said one thing but really meant something else? Of course there are figures of speech, especially in the poetic and prophetic books,

169

which must be recognized for what they are, but as with other books the Bible should be read literally. According to Ramm, all parables, types, allegories, symbols, figures of speech, myths, and fables are based on and refer to literal speech. The symbolism of a lion, for example, is based upon what is asserted about lions in literal speech.[10] Many heresies and fanciful interpretations of the Bible could have been avoided if readers had started with the clearly literal statements of the Bible and referred all figures of speech back to them.

According to the new foundation we have been proposing, the Bible is not seen as just another book of literature. It is the Word of God, divinely inspired and without error in its original form. It is the verbal means by which a living God speaks to men and women today. Just as a highly sophisticated psychology book will be best understood by someone who is familiar with psychology, so the book that deals with spiritual matters is understood with clarity only by the spiritual man or woman.[11] It has been suggested, therefore, that really to comprehend the Bible one must be "born again" (that is, become part of the group who have invited Christ to control their lives), deeply respectful of God, highly desirous of knowing God, and completely dependent on the Holy Spirit to guide one's interpretation.[12]

In addition to these issues about the nature of man and his universe, scientific methodology, and the problem of biblical interpretation, the new psychology gives rise to the problem of integration between psychology and theology. The proposed new foundation is built on the premise that God has revealed himself through a natural world, discoverable by science, and through the Bible, interpreted by hermeneutics and understood by theology. Presumably the findings of psychology and theology, if they are valid, should not be in contradiction since they are two perspectives on the same body of truth. As we have seen in chapter 6, however, there is often contradiction and disagreement between psychology and

170   theology, so much so that even Christians sometimes
question whether integration between the two fields is
possible. Psychology and theology both deal with
human behavior, values, interpersonal relations, attitudes,
pathology, and counseling, but the two approaches have
used different language, employed different methods, and
held different viewpoints about the universe. To confuse
matters further, both fields are complex, containing a
variety of approaches and systems. Psychologists don't
always agree with each other and neither do theologians.
It is hardly surprising, therefore, that psychologists and
theologians have difficulty understanding, communicating,
and agreeing with each other.

Over the years, in spite of these difficulties there have
been various approaches to integration. Some have tried
to explain away the disagreements between psychology
and theology, claiming that the problems are more
apparent than real.[13] Others have taken a
question-and-answer approach, maintaining that
psychology or theology asks questions for the other field to
answer. Some have taken a linguistic approach,
attempting to align concepts in psychology (superego, id,
mental health, or self-actualization) with somewhat
parallel ideas in theology (conscience, sin, spiritual
maturity, or sanctification). A more sophisticated version
of this has been the "models" approach, in which major
subsections of systematic theology are paralleled with
subfields of psychology (e.g., theology proper = the science
of psychology; angelology = psychic phenomena;
anthropology = personality; soteriology = development;
ecclesiology = social psychology; etc.).[14] More
common has been a topical approach, in which issues such
as conversion, faith healing, guilt, or miracles are
analyzed from both psychological and theological
perspectives. Paul Meehl has stated this approach
concisely in the beginning of a well-respected book on
psychology and theology:

We are prepared to state firmly that he who does

not come to terms with such theoretical problems as determinism, guilt, original sin, materialism, monism, conscience, and conversion cannot even begin to work out a cognitive rapprochement between Christian theology and the secular sciences of behavior.[15]

In a book on science and Christian faith, Richard Bube has presented what might be called a "levels of description" approach to integration. This approach begins with two major theses:

Thesis I. The universe exists moment by moment only because of the creative and preserving power of God.
Thesis II. There are many levels at which a given situation can be described. An exhaustive description on one level does not preclude meaningful descriptions on other levels.[16]

The first of these theses is consistent with the view of the universe taken earlier in this chapter. It assumes that it is meaningless to talk of a God who works through natural laws, intervenes in the natural order, or is able to ignore natural laws. God created the natural laws and they exist only because he is constantly active in upholding them.[17]

The second thesis assumes that any one event or phenomenon can be described or analyzed at a variety of levels. A religious conversion, for example, could be described in the language of physiology, psychology, sociology, or theology. One might say, for example, that at the time of conversion, the convert had a reaction in the brain (physiological), that he experienced "closure" or the sudden fulfillment of needs (psychological), that he was swayed by group pressure (sociological), or that God intervened to change his life (theological). Regretfully, such descriptions can lead to the error of nothing buttery (e.g., conversion is nothing but a response to social

172 pressure); it would be more accurate to say that conversion can be explained at all four levels (and probably more). According to this view, therefore, descriptions on every level can be valid and meaningful, so it is neither proper nor necessary to exclude descriptions at some other level. Some levels may give a more precise explanation of an event than do others, but it would be illogical to assume, for example, that the biblical explanation of some event disproves the psychological explanation, or that the psychological (physiological, chemical, or other) explanation disproves the theological. Both theological and scientific explanations can be simultaneously valid or invalid. Complete knowledge requires an exhaustive description on every level.

Figure 3 is a portrayal of the different levels of description in the universe as proposed by Bube. As we ascend the scale we see that the higher levels are broader in scope and more embracing than the lower levels. Consider, for example, the middle column of figure 3. Energy, which is basic to all creation, forms elementary subatomic particles which interact to form atoms, then molecules, then nonliving matter. As these elements continue to interact, cellular life emerges, then plants and animals. To look at the picture from the opposite point of view, all plants consist of cells, and cells are composed of nonliving molecules and atoms.

In Figure 3 there is a sharp line between the Creator and the creation which God made and sustains. He is above all and over all. To catch a glimpse of the Creator (so far as our finite minds can comprehend) we utilize the methods of theology and biblical hermeneutics; to understand the created order we utilize the methods of science and the humanities.

There are several reasons why it is difficult to integrate psychology and theology. The psychologist may attempt to make his scientific interpretations of the natural world preeminent over the theologian's interpretations of revelation, or the theologian may attempt to do the reverse.[18] Either may deny the validity of the other's explanation or proclaim that his own explanation is superior. Conflict and mutual distrust often follow. In addition, there are variations in the terminology and concepts used at different levels of description. These create difficulties in communication and raise obstacles to mutual understanding.

Much of the integration problem arises, however, because psychologists and theologians suspect that integration might be the same as obliteration. Some may have pondered this question while reading this book. If psychology is built on a biblical, God-centered foundation, isn't there danger of its being swallowed up by theology? Might it not be better for psychologists and theologians to stay within the borders of their respective fields or levels of interpretation, especially when the boundary lines between psychology and theology are already so hazy in spots?[19]

The proposed new foundation for psychology does much to pull together the fields of psychology and theology. Because of the resulting exposure to new facts, each of the two fields stands to benefit from coming together, but there is enough uniqueness in each field to prevent the elimination of either.

Much modern psychology already reflects and is based on theological and philosophical values, assumptions, and beliefs. To deny this or to ignore it does not change the reality of the situation. Thus, psychologists would do better to recognize the philosophical and theological bases of their discipline and then go on to fulfill their unique function: studying God's *natural* revelation as seen in human behavior and functioning. Such study should use a variety of techniques including empirical scientific methods, analysis of subjective experiences, logical deduction, study of literature and the arts, etc. Familiarity with the Bible can greatly facilitate the psychologist's understanding of man and his behavior.

Similarly, it must be recognized that theology already reflects and is based on much human insight, personal

174 needs, cultural relativism, and the perceptual perspectives of the theologian. To deny this or to ignore it does not change the fact of the human influence on theological work. Theologians would be wise to recognize the psychological and sociological impact on their discipline and then go on to fulfill their unique function: studying God's *special* revelation as recorded in the Bible and as uncovered by hermeneutical techniques. Familiarity with psychology can surely increase the theologian's understanding of the parables, the actions of Bible characters, and the teachings of Scripture concerning man.

Figure 3:
Levels of Description.
Events and phenomena in the universe can be studied at a variety of levels. The most basic level is at the bottom of the chart. Each higher level in God's creation includes the subject matter which is below. An exhaustive description at one level does not rule out meaningful descriptions at other levels. (Adapted from Bube, 1971, p. 34.)

	Area of Study	Subject Matter	Discipline
The Creator	Ultimate	God	Theology
The Creation	Human	Society Man	Sociology Anthropology Psychology
	Living but nonhuman	Animals Plants	Zoology Botany
	Simple life	Cell	Biology
	Material but nonliving	Nonliving matter Molecules Atoms Elementary particles	Physics Chemistry
	Nonmaterial	Energy	Origins

At times, of course, the findings of psychology and the truths of the Bible will appear to be so much in contradiction that integration will seem impossible. On such occasions, the individual

> takes it for granted that revelation cannot genuinely contradict any truth about man or the world which is discoverable by other means (including science.) If such appears to have happened, he must operate on the assumption that this is only an appearance. That being presupposed, he then seeks to resolve the contradiction....If the resolution cannot be effected, the problem is put on the shelf as a mystery, not solvable by the lights of nature or of grace but only by the light of glory.[20]

What, then, would be the shape of a psychology or psychologies built on a biblical foundation? As a minimum, we propose that such a psychology would:

—be alert to and continually questioning the nature and influence of its underlying foundation and presuppositions;

—accept a view of the universe that acknowledges the existence of God both as the Creator and Sustainer of everything (including man) and as the Author of all truth;

—acknowledge that since all truth comes from God, both natural and special revelation are part of a unified, integrated, and noncontradictory whole;

—study God's human creation using every technique available, including (but not limited to) scientific empirical methods and study of the Bible;

—view man as a unique, special, and holistic-unified creation of God, a being who deliberately rebelled against the Creator, whose return to communion and fellowship with God is based solely upon divine love and grace, and who exists in two broad categories: natural and redeemed;

—develop a view of pathology and a form of counseling consistent with and based upon the truths of Scripture and the findings of psychological research;

—be open to continual reexamination and reevaluation of itself as new facts are uncovered; and

176   —evaluate current and future psychological findings
not only for their logical and empirical support, but also
for their philosophical foundations and consistency with
the truths of special revelation as found in the Bible.

In an earlier chapter we observed that psychology is
fragmented and overspecialized. At present, general
psychology textbooks are filled with small pieces of
information, very little of which fits together in any
systematic way. If we assume, however, that all truth
originates with God and that all truth will be consistent
with the revealed Word of God as found in the Bible, then
we have a central core around which everything fits. The
Bible does not address itself to all of the issues that
concern psychology—or even to most of them—but the
Bible does provide us with a comprehensive and
self-consistent world view into which we can begin to fit
the facts of psychology as they become more available.
Much of the ambiguity, uncertainty, and contradiction
in psychology thus disappears. There is a new basis for
values and a new standard on which to build our ethical
system. If we assume, further, that special (i.e., biblical)
revelation is the true Word of God, then we also have a
measure against which we can ultimately test our scientific
conclusions. All truth, including what is discovered by
psychological science, must be consistent with the truth
of biblical revelation.

The new biblically-based foundation also helps to deal
with a problem unique to the social sciences. This is the
problem of the observer being a part of his own subject
matter, which is not an issue in natural science. The
biologist who studies amoebae, the botanist who studies
African violets, the geologist who studies moon rocks
can all look at their subject matter with at least some
objectivity. These scientists are not amoebae, plants, or
rocks. But the social scientist does not have the same
privilege. He studies man of whom he is one. This makes
objectivity exceptionally difficult unless we can somehow
get a superhuman view of mankind against which to test
our conclusions. We need a Being outside of man, a

177

transhuman Being, who is able to give a perspective that no human observer can get on his own. The Christian believes that this is what God has done in the Bible. It is not a scientific text, but it says things about man and his nature that the psychologist could never discover using the techniques of empirical science alone to look at himself. To brush aside the biblical data is to ignore a unique body of information of great significance in any study of man and his world.

If we begin to test our scientific findings against the book through which the existing God has revealed himself, then we are likely to become more issue-oriented and less method-centered. We might even find ourselves becoming more relevant and less concerned about picayune issues, more concerned with creative ideas and less worried about the psychological respectability or publishability of our ideas, more willing to consider data from a variety of sources and less bound to what can be operationally defined or statistically measured, more interested in people and less concerned about rats and pigeons.

But what about highly specialized research, studies of monkeys and earthworms or theorizing about minute aspects of man's personality and behavior? Must all of this be abandoned if we accept the new foundation for psychology? The answer is "no." The fine points of such issues as how a white rat progresses through a maze or the influence of reactive inhibition in the learning of skills certainly are legitimate topics for study. But with the new working assumptions of modified reductionism or biblical anthropology (or with the concept of levels of description), we will be much less inclined to generalize from animals to humans or from a study of parts to an understanding of the whole man. Rat studies tell us about rats, but they say little about men and women who are created in God's image.

Footnotes
Chapter 9

[1]Schultz, Duane P. (ed.). *The Science of Psychology: Critical Reflections.* New York: Appleton-Century-Crofts, 1970, p. 393.

178

[2]*Ibid.*, p. 394.

[3]Reported in Pinnock, Clark H., *Set Forth Your Case*. Chicago: Moody Press, 1967, p. 102.

[4]Carnell, Edward J. *An Introduction to Christian Apologetics*. Grand Rapids: Eerdmans, 1948, p. 210.

[5]Colossians 1:16, 17.

[6]2 Corinthians 5:17; 1 Corinthians 2:14-16; Galatians 5:22-26; John 2:16.

[7]Platt, John R. "Strong Inference," *Science* **146,** October, 1964, pp. 347-52.

[8]Crabb, Lawrence J., "Data and Dogma are Compatible," *Christianity Today* **15,** March 12, 1971, pp. 7, 8.

[9]Ramm, B. *Protestant Biblical Interpretation* (third revised ed.) Grand Rapids, Baker, 1970, p. 105.

[10]*Ibid.*, p. 124.

[11]1 Corinthians 2:14, 15.

[12]Ramm, *op. cit.*, pp. 12, 13.

[13]See, for example, Tournier, Paul, *A Place for You*. New York: Harper & Row, 1968, pp. 92-3.

[14]Carter, J. D., and Mohline, R. J. "A Model and Models for the Integrative Process." Paper presented at the annual meeting of the Christian Association for Psychological Studies, Oklahoma City, April 12, 1975.

[15]Meehl, P. *et al. What, Then, Is Man?* St. Louis: Concordia, 1958, p. 5.

[16]Bube, R. H. *The Human Quest*. Waco, Texas: Word, 1971, p. 26.

[17]Hebrews 1:3; Colossians 1:16, 17; Job 12:10; 1 Corinthians 8:16; Acts 17:28.

[18]Bube, *op. cit.*, p. 71.

[19]Stackhouse, M. L. "On the Boundary of Psychology and Theology." Address given to the Northeast Regional Convention of the Association of Clinical Pastoral Educators, Waltham, Mass., July 19-20, 1974.

[20]Meehl, *op. cit.*, p. 181.

Chapter Ten

PSYCHOLOGY

IN
DISCIPLESHIP
COUNSELING

IN the preceding chapters of this book, little has been said about how, or even if, the proposed new foundation for psychology could be used to change human behavior.

How, one might ask, would a biblically-based psychology work in practice?

What would be its goals?

How would it help those in need of counsel?

There might be sound logical reasons for introducing a new foundation for psychology, but if the new foundation does not in fact remove some of psychology's problems and set it on a new course, if it does not at least give a different perspective to current practice, we are simply replacing one ineffective system with another.

Nowhere are these questions of greater importance than in the area of counseling. Any approach to counseling must begin with a view of abnormality (why people have problems), move to consideration of the goals of counseling, and then discuss therapeutic techniques.

In this chapter we will deal with these three issues, working from the assumption that God, who exists, may have revealed something about each of these matters in the Bible and/or in psychology.

In the past, many approaches to the study of abnormality have oversimplified human behavior to the point of suggesting that all human problems can be explained by one or two causes. Within the field of psychology and psychiatry, for example, we have those who reduce all problems to a lack of meaning in life, to a sense of inferiority, to faulty learning, or to anxiety. One of the most interesting examples of this kind of reductionism is a system recently proposed by a theologian who began with a rejection of psychology, erroneously concluded that the Bible is a textbook of psychiatry, and concluded from his hermeneutical studies that personal sin and physical disease were the only two possible causes for human problems.[1]

Most professional counselors do not take such a narrow and indefensible view. Abundant scientific

182   evidence shows that psychological abnormality can be caused by a variety of physical causes (such as brain damage, physical infection and disease, genetic malfunctioning, deprivation of sleep or oxygen), psychological factors (like faulty learning, traumatic past experiences, internal conflicts), and social influences (such as the breakup of a marriage, the loss of one's job, the destruction of one's home in a tornado). These and other influences can combine to put so much pressure on an individual that he or she breaks down under stress.[2]

The Christian psychologist acknowledges that a variety of causes for psychopathology have been discovered by scientific investigation. In addition, he or she maintains that the Bible also has something to say about human problems, including why the problems began in the first place. When first created, man was in a utopian environment, but after the fall into disobedience, was condemned to a life of physical and psychological hardship. Thus sin became the root cause of all subsequent problems. Man's sinful state not only gave rise to harmful physiological, psychological, and social influences, it also led to destructive spiritual behaviors, better known as individual sins. These sins—which include such things as greed, backbiting, stealing, immoral sexual behavior, or ignoring God, to name a few—reflect our sinful nature, express our rebellion against God, and can, along with the physiological, psychological, and social influences, create emotional difficulties.

Most psychological definitions of abnormality or psychopathology refer to social behavior. Persons are judged to be "abnormal," for example, if their behavior is at odds with the expectations of the society in which they live. The murderer, hermit, paranoid schizophrenic, and sex deviate are "abnormal" because their behavior is unusual or nontypical when compared with people around them. In addition, textbook writers frequently define abnormality with reference to psychological

183

functioning. Persons who in every respect behave normally are still assumed to be disturbed or at least somewhat abnormal if they experience internal conflicts leading to intense and prolonged feelings of insecurity, guilt, anxiety, or unhappiness. Many practitioners would also assume that psychological abnormality is present if a disease or other organ malfunction interferes with an individual's maximal psychological functioning.

In addition to these social, psychological, and physical criteria, the new approach to counseling would propose that a person is abnormal if he is alienated from God. Man was created in the divine image, and made for communion with his Maker. When he rebelled, man became separated from God. This separation is abnormal. Since by our own efforts we cannot reestablish this closeness, a divine provision was made which permits anyone who so desires to come back to God. Individuals are returned to a state of oneness with the Creator when they acknowledge their sinful separation from God, believe in the resurrection of Jesus Christ, and accept him as Lord of their lives.[3] This restoration is normal. It is the ideal that God wants for all human beings regardless of cultural background.

Most modern textbooks of psychology would accept the social, psychological, and perhaps the physical definitions of psychopathology, but few would accept the spiritual definition. All four are important, however, and it is unlikely that people can ever be really at peace with their society and with themselves until they are at peace with God. By defining abnormality in so many ways we are suggesting that it is rare, and sometimes impossible, for a person to be completely normal.

It should not be assumed, however, that this fourfold definition of abnormality implies that man is divisible into separate parts. G. C. Berkouwer, the Dutch theologian, has argued that to divide man into two, three, or more parts is a carryover from Greek philosophy and is not supported by the Bible. "The biblical view of man," Berkouwer has written

...shows him to us in an impressive diversity, but...it never loses sight of the unity of the whole man.... It appears clearly, then, that Scripture never pictures man as a dualistic, or pluralistic being, but that in all its varied expressions the whole man comes to the fore, in all his guilt and sin, his need and oppression, his longings and his nostalgia.[4]

No problem is strictly psychological or social, purely physical, or "simply spiritual." When something goes wrong with one part of a unified person, the individual's whole being is affected. A doctor may specialize in treating some part of the body such as ear, nose, and throat, or urinary tract; he may have expertise in dealing with some specialized psychological problem like schizophrenia or learning difficulties; he may be a pastoral counselor whose main interest is with spiritual healing. But all counselors must remember that there is no sharp line between the spiritual, the social, the emotional-cognitive-behavioral-psychological, and the physical person. One or two symptoms may predominate and cry for help, but at such a time the entire body is off balance. Our helping will be more effective if we do not lose sight of the holistic nature of man.

In an earlier work,[5] counseling was defined as a relationship between two or more persons in which one person, the counselor, seeks to help another person or persons, the counselee(s), to deal more effectively with the problems of life. Counseling may have a number of goals, including a changing of the counselee's behavior, attitudes, or values; the teaching of social skills; encouraging the expression of emotions; giving support in times of need; instilling insight; preventing more serious problems from developing; helping the counselee to meet his needs; guiding him as a decision is made; teaching responsibility; stimulating spiritual and personal growth; encouraging him to confess sin; or helping him to mobilize inner resources in times of crisis. To accomplish these goals, various counseling techniques and schools of psychotherapy have been developed, all of which have their enthusiastic advocates.

At the risk of oversimplification it is possible to place the various theoretical counseling approaches on a directive-permissive continuum.[6] Starting at the directive end we see the rational-emotive therapy of Ellis. Farther along are the learning and behavior therapies, the various analytic systems, the reality therapy of Glasser, and the helping approach of Brammer who suggests that the counselor and counselee are colleagues working on a problem together. More toward the permissive end of the scale are the client-centered therapy of Rogers, the self or phenomenological approaches, and the Gestalt, encounter, and experiential therapies.

Parallel to this continuum have been a number of Christian approaches to counseling. At the directive end is the nouthetic counseling of Jay Adams. Paul Tournier's "dialogue counseling" is in the middle. Some of the early Rogerian-based approaches to pastoral counseling are at the permissive end. As with the secular systems, the proponents of these Christian approaches (Tournier excepted) generally maintain that their particular approach is the most effective, but they also see their approach as the most biblically and theologically sound.

A careful look at the Bible reveals, however, that a variety of techniques were used when counseling took place. Jesus, for example, held rational discussions with the confused Nicodemus, encouraged and supported people like John the Baptist in prison, criticized and dealt directly with the religious hypocrites of his day, confronted the woman at the well with her immorality, gently forgave the woman taken in adultery, listened nondirectively to the two on the road to Emmaus and then taught them from the Scriptures. It could be argued that these were not really counseling situations. None of them occurred in a clinic, there was no fee, no fifty-minute hour, and no diplomas hanging on the wall. Nevertheless, Jesus was dealing with people in distress, and his

186

techniques illustrate that he was not bound to any one directive, interactional, or permissive approach.

In all of his contacts with people, however, Jesus had one goal in mind: to make disciples. Minutes before ascending into heaven, Jesus summarized his earthly ministry and message when he issued what has come to be known as the Great Commission. "All authority has been given to Me in heaven and on earth," he stated. "Go therefore and make disciples of all nations, baptizing them in the name of the Father and the Son and the Holy Spirit, teaching them to observe all that I commanded you; and lo, I am with you always, even to the end of the age." It was a twofold directive: to win men and women to Christ, and to teach them so that they in turn could be disciples and disciplers. The Great Commission was not restricted to those who stood with Jesus on the mountain near Jerusalem. It was a challenge to every believer, including Christian counselors in the centuries that were still to come.

It is possible, no doubt, to build a number of biblically-based approaches to counseling: approaches acknowledging that God exists and has revealed truth both through psychology and through the Bible. Such approaches utilize scientific methods and established counseling techniques; they also apply biblical teachings to the counseling relationship and, following the example of Jesus, utilize a variety of therapeutic methods. To be truly biblical, however, an approach to counseling must take the Great Commission seriously and place the discipling of men and women at its core.

Such a conclusion is likely to be resisted, even by many Christian counselors. We have been taught to remain neutral in a counseling situation, to keep values hidden and refrain from imposing our philosophical or theological conclusions on the counselee. It is true, of course, that the integrity and freedom of counselees must be respected, but the Christian no more hides his values than does Ellis, Rogers, Glasser, or any other therapist. To hide one's Christian commitment is

187

dishonest, ultimately unfair, and even harmful to the counselee with whom we are trying to build an honest, open relationship.

Discipleship Counseling[7] is the name that we might give to a biblically-based approach, built on the foundation that has been proposed in the previous pages of this book, and alert to the Great Commission. Discipleship Counseling has as its goal the helping of counselees to function effectively in the society in which they live, to be at peace with themselves, to be in communion with God, and to be actively involved in becoming disciples of and disciplers for Jesus Christ. Although social and psychological harmony are desirable goals in themselves, human beings cannot really be at peace with the world and with themselves until they have established a personal relationship with God. It is then that a person becomes a new creation who is able to actualize his or her complete potential, find purpose in existence, and fully develop God-given gifts and abilities. Discipleship Counseling has six principles, each of which is consistent both with God's special revelation as revealed in the Bible and with God's general revelation as revealed in nature and discovered by scientific psychology.

1. In any counseling relationship, the personality, values, attitudes, and beliefs of the counselor are of prime importance. Stated differently, the place to begin effective counseling is with the counselor. Perhaps no principle of counseling has been better established by empirical research. Truax and his colleagues,[8] for example, have concluded that two out of every three therapists are either ineffective or harmful. Those who are successful succeed not so much because of their theoretical orientation or techniques; they succeed because they possess at least three personality characteristics: empathic understanding, nonpossessive warmth, and genuineness.

Counseling is most likely to be successful when love and

188

compassion are present. More than any other individual who walked the earth, Jesus showed compassion for people. He came to earth in the first place because of divine love, and he expects that his followers will be characterized by the kind of love described in the Bible.[9] Love has been described as the mark of a Christian disciple;[10] it is also the mark of a successful counselor.

In the biblical book of Galatians, the readers are instructed to counsel with those who have slipped into sinful problems or broken human relationships. The counselor (restorer) is expected to be an individual who is "spiritual"—characterized by love, joy, peace, patience, kindness, goodness, faithfulness, gentleness, self-control, and a humble, realistic self-image.[11] This is not to suggest that the spiritual individual is automatically an effective counselor or that the nonspiritual counselor is ineffective. It is clear, however, that the Bible and secular psychology both recognize the prime importance of the counselor's personality in facilitating the counseling process. Both would agree that effective counseling characteristics and skills can be developed. The biblically-based approach would maintain, in addition, that the Holy Spirit of God can instill these traits in the follower of Christ.

2. The counselee's attitude and desire for improvement is a significant variable. Research has shown that counselees are less likely to improve when they are resistant to counseling, unwilling, not expecting to get better, or lacking confidence in the counselor or counseling process.[12] Even Jesus failed to help people who resisted his counsel. The rich young ruler, for example, presented a problem, heard Jesus' counsel, and walked away. Both the traditional psychological and biblically-based approaches agree that a counselee's resistance has to be dealt with early in the course of counseling.

3. In counseling, the helping relationship between counselor and counselee is of great importance. As every student knows, good rapport is essential for successful

189 counseling. However, the relationship between counselor and counselee can vary considerably, depending on the personality or competence of the counselor and on the characteristics or problems of the counselee. Jesus, for example, had different relationships with John ("the disciple whom he loved"), the impulsive burly Peter, Zacchaeus who was in a tree when he first met the Master, Mary and Martha in whose home Jesus often stayed, or the woman with the issue of blood who met the Lord only briefly in the midst of a jostling crowd.

It should be noted, too, that Jesus sometimes talked with people alone, yet at other times he met with groups. Some contemporary group therapy encourages behavior that is unbiblical and hence must be rejected, but there is nothing in the Bible to suggest that group counseling *per se* is harmful, ineffective, or wrong. Indeed, the Bible emphasizes one aspect of counseling that has been overlooked by some contemporary psychologists: the importance of a supportive therapeutic community. Individual counseling (*i.e.*, two people working alone) can be helpful—research and experience have shown that—but the encouragement and help of a supportive group, such as a church, can add to the effectiveness of a counseling relationship.

The church is pictured in the Bible as a body with various parts.[13] Some parts are more prominent than others, but all are needed. In order to survive, each needs the life-giving vitality that comes from being "attached" to the rest of the body. Individuals are like these parts. Without contact and support from others we wither and die, psychologically if not physically.

According to the Bible there should be a mutual bearing of burdens among the members of the body,[14] perhaps even between a counselor and counselee. The counselee is the one who comes with the problem, of course, and the counseling relationship is more than just a chat between friends. But if the counselor is honest enough to share that he too has problems in life, the counseling relationship is deepened, improvement can be

190   facilitated, and the counselor's skills become more effective in bringing change. Admittedly the church often fails in its supportive function, but such support must be part of a biblically-based approach.

4. Counseling must acknowledge the joint relevance of subjective inner emotions, cognitive thought processes, and overt behavior. Stated more simply, feelings, thoughts, and actions are all important aspects of human functioning and must all be considered in counseling. Many of the prevalent approaches emphasize one or two of these factors almost to the exclusion of the others. Rogers and the permissive approaches, for example, put greatest emphasis on feelings; Ellis, while acknowledging the relevance of all three, nevertheless deals almost exclusively with the rational; Jay Adams and the behavior therapies virtually ignore feelings and focus on behavior—specifically ineffective, harmful, or (in the system of Dr. Adams) sinful behavior.

In any given counseling situation it may be that the counselor will emphasize feeling, thought, or behavior, but according to the Bible all three are of great importance. Jesus never denied feelings, hid his own emotions, or condemned people for expressing their feelings. He cried at the graveside of Lazarus and wept as he looked over Jerusalem. But he also emphasized thinking. His counseling with Nicodemus took the form of an intellectual debate over apologetics. In response to the doubts of both John the Baptist and Thomas, Jesus presented each with the rational evidence they sought. On other occasions he was concerned with sin and overt behavior, especially when, as with people like Zacchaeus or the woman taken in adultery, it was causing human problems.

5. Counseling must utilize a variety of techniques. The Bible does not support the idea that counseling must always be directive, nondirective, or fitting in some other mold. Jesus used a variety of techniques, depending on the problem being presented. At different times he was supportive, confrontational, directive, educative, and

nondirective. The writers of the epistles followed his example. In the sixth chapter of his letter to the church at Galatia the Apostle Paul instructed the spiritual counselor to restore sinners to a state of reconciliation with God and with others (verse 1), to bear burdens in a spirit of mutual concern (verse 2), to examine his own life and work continually (verses 3 and 4), to teach, learn from, and even receive money from his counselees (verse 6). He emphasized the importance of personal responsibility (verses 7 and 8) and urged them to persist in the counseling task even when the work is difficult (verse 9), trying to help everyone, but especially those who are believers (verse 10). The Bible never claims to be a textbook of counseling and it should not be viewed as such. Nevertheless, it does say a great deal about human nature, interpersonal relations, and behavior change. Counseling methods, therefore, should not only be examined scientifically; they should be held up to the searching light of biblical authority. Any technique that contradicts biblical teaching or advocates behavior opposed by Scripture must be rejected, regardless of its supposed therapeutic effectiveness. Scientific validity, pragmatic effectiveness, and consistency with the principles of biblical revelation all become standards, then, against which our techniques are examined.

6. The ultimate goal of biblically-based counseling is to make disciples and disciplers. Each of the preceding five principles might be acceptable, more or less, to contemporary professional counselors, but this principle is uniquely biblical and likely to be resisted. Consider, however, the example of a Christian physician who is confronted with a patient in pain. Like every other Christian, he has a responsibility to make disciples, but like Jesus, the physician starts where his patient is hurting. He tends wounds, gives medicine, does the needed surgery, or may give only a cup of cold water, but in so doing the doctor demonstrates the love of Christ through his action and concern. At some time the physician may talk openly about spiritual matters and he may even lead

the patient to Christ or contribute to his or her spiritual pilgrimage in some other way. This is the Christian doctor's ultimate goal—the healing of body, mind and spirit—but he knows that he will not accomplish all of this with every patient.

In the discipling process an individual goes through several steps. He first must come in contact with someone who can present the gospel message; he must make the decision to commit his life to Christ (conversion); he must begin to mature as a Christian (a lifelong process); and he must start the process of discipling others. The Christian counselor may influence a life at any stage in this process. He may help a nonbeliever with a problem and never have opportunity to discuss spiritual matters, or he may discuss spiritual issues with a counselee who in turn may either reject the message or come to the point of conversion. At other times the counselor may help a mature believer who has spent many years discipling others but now needs help with a personal problem. Sometimes the counselor works with his counselee for a long period of time, for many months or even years. On other occasions the counselor has contact with a person for a brief period, is instrumental in bringing about some change, and then the two of them go in separate directions. The counselor who takes the Bible seriously has two major goals in life: to be a disciple of Jesus Christ and to make disciples of others. To be a disciple is to be more sensitive, loving, and self-actualized. In short, to be a better counselor is to be a model and teacher, demonstrating to the counselee how life as a disciple should be lived. To make disciples is to help men, women, and children reach a state of wholeness and personal integration, which comes as the result of their commitment to Jesus Christ.

Religiously motivated counselors often assume that their only goal is to bring about the counselee's conversion, with the assumption that the spiritual change is all that really matters. The Bible, however, emphasizes the importance of good interpersonal relations, psychological stability, and physical healing. These, then, must concern the counselor as much as the spiritual welfare of the counselee. If man is the holistic creature that we propose, change in one of these areas invariably influences the other areas of life.

The new foundation for psychology, therefore, broadens our understanding of psychological disturbance (since it acknowledges the influence of spiritual as well as physical, psychological, and social causes of psychopathology) and leads to additional techniques (such as prayer or scriptural meditation) for dealing with personal problems.[15] It should not be concluded that the Christian counselor believes all mental illness to be caused by sin and satanic forces, or that prayer and increased faith will inevitably make all things better; but neither are these influences dismissed as being irrelevant or of no concern. The Christian does not conclude that religion is always harmful to a counselee, but neither does he proclaim that one's beliefs are always beneficial since it is well documented that some people misconstrue the biblical message and develop an unhealthy, immature, and self-defeating faith.[16] The competent Christian counselor does not preach to his patients or coerce them into accepting a given system of values, but neither does he blithely assume that all values are relative, that one set of beliefs is just as good as any other, or that values and religious matters are to be ignored in the helping relationship.

The new foundation for psychology lets us make use of a variety of therapeutic tools and established skills, but it also permits, and indeed requires, the therapist and his patient to be aware of God's existence and to consider his relevance to the therapeutic process. We recognize that some things in life are determined, but that man has also been given a large measure of free will and individual responsibility. We acknowledge that people are biological organisms whose behavior and emotions largely depend on their individual physiology and environmental influences. But people are also unique beings who have

194

a measure of self-determination, are directly influenced at times by supernatural forces, are freed from sin's penalty by Jesus Christ, are protected by a loving God, and are guided by his Holy Spirit.

Even though clinical psychologists have tended to be critical of religion, some counselors have always recognized the value of theology. Many years ago Rollo May concluded that "psychotherapy needs theology"[17] and men like Jung, Mowrer, or Frankl might be inclined to agree. Harvard psychologist Gordon Allport, who to my knowledge never claimed to be a Christian, once wrote an influential little book in which he proposed that clinical psychology needed to be aware of the healing power of religion.

Consider, for example, the place of love in therapy. According to Allport:

> Love—incomparably the greatest psychotherapeutic agent—is something that professional psychiatry (or psychology) cannot of itself create, focus, nor release.... Psychotherapy knows the healing power of love, but finds itself unable to do much about it....
>
> By contrast, religion—especially the Christian religion—offers an interpretation of life and a rule of life based wholly upon love. It calls attention again and again to this fundamental groundwork. On love for God and man "hang all the Law and the Prophets." The emphasis is insistent: "Beloved, let us love one another: for love is of God; and everyone that loveth is born of God, and knoweth God. He that loveth not knoweth not God: for God is love." (1 John 4:7, 8)
>
> Perhaps the very insistence of religion in this matter is in part responsible for the "tenderness tabu" that has descended upon psychology. Having rejected the religious approach to the cure of souls, science regards it as more realistic to center attention upon...hate, aggression, compulsive

sexuality—even if these are merely pathological conditions due to deprivation of love.[18]

As Allport indicates, love is not only a powerful therapeutic tool; it is a basic tenet of Christian faith. The Bible not only describes love and proclaims that love is the best antidote to fear,[19] but it tells us how God showed his love to mankind. "God showed how much he loved us by sending his only Son into this wicked world to bring us eternal life through his death. In this act we see what real love is: it is not our love for God, but his love for us when he sent his Son to satisfy God's anger against our sins." Such love demands more than intellectual admiration. "Since God loved us as much as that, we surely ought to love each other too"[20] and to commit our lives to divine control. "For God loved the world so much that he gave his only Son so that anyone who believes in him shall not perish but have eternal life."[21]

As we saw in chapter 3, psychotherapy on its old foundation has helped many people even though it has weaknesses. To extend clinical psychology to include religious insights could make our counseling work even more effective. But our proposed new foundation does not simply urge that psychologists give sympathetic attention to religion in general. We are proposing something more radical: that psychologists and psychology students themselves commit their lives to the Christ of the Bible and find both meaning for life and guidelines for behavior in God's written revelation to man. Christ's so-called "Sermon on the Mount" is one example of a gold mine of practical direction for life.[22] So filled is this message with practical insights about man and his behavior that even Mahatma Gandhi, while rejecting most of traditional Christianity, nevertheless read this sermon almost every day until the time of his assassination.[23] When applied to the life of the counselor who is a committed disciple of Jesus Christ, biblical insights could have a significant impact on effectiveness in counseling.

196   In the preceding pages we have tried to show that
modern psychology may be ailing, but it most certainly
is not dead. Its past may have been less productive than we
might have wished, but its future is bright and filled with
hope. There may have been a time when psychologists
refused to face the weaknesses of their profession, but
we have now launched into an era of healthy
self-examination and creative attempts at self-
improvement. At long last we are moving away from
the behavioristic and naturalistic restraints of the past
and into a reevaluation of our foundations. It is time for us
to realize that psychology will be strongest in the future
if it dares to acknowledge God and to build on a theistic
undergirding. Only then will psychology be able to
realize its maximum effectiveness in understanding
mankind and helping the world to be a better place in
which to live.

Footnotes
Chapter 10

[1]Adams, Jay E. *Competent to Counsel.* Grand Rapids: Baker, 1970.
[2]For a further discussion of the scientific causes of abnormality see
Coleman, J. C., and Broen, W., *Abnormal Psychology and Modern
Life.* 4th ed. Glenview: Scott, Foresman, 1972.
[3]Romans 10:9. This discussion is adapted from the author's earlier
work, *Search for Reality: Psychology and the Christian.* Santa Ana,
California: Vision House, 1969.
[4]Berkouwer, G. C. *Man: The Image of God.* Grand Rapids: Eerdmans,
1962, p. 200, 203.
[5]Collins, G. R. *Effective Counseling.* Carol Stream, Illinois: Creation
House, 1972, pp. 13, 14.
[6]This continuum is suggested by C. H. Patterson, *Theories of Counseling
and Psychotherapy,* (2nd ed.). New York: Harper & Row, 1973.
[7]For a more detailed discussion of discipleship counseling, see Gary R.
Collins, *How to Be a People Helper.* Santa Ana, California: Vision
House, 1976.
[8]Truax, C. B. and Carkhuff, R. R. *Toward Effective Counseling and
Psychotherapy: Training and Practice.* Chicago: Aldine, 1967; Truax,
C. B. and Mitchell, K. M. "Research on certain therapist
interpersonal skills in relation to process and outcome." In A. E. Bergin
and S. L. Garfield (eds.), *Handbook of Psychotherapy and Behavior
Change: An Empirical Analysis.* New York: Wiley, 1971, p. 299-344.
[9]1 Corinthians 13; Matthew 22:39; John 13:35, 15:9, 12.
[10]Schaeffer, F. A. *The Church at the End of the Twentieth Century.*
Downers Grove, Illinois: Inter-Varsity, 1970.
[11]See Galatians 5:1. The characteristics cited are those of the spiritual
individual described in Galatians 5:22-26.

197

[12]Bergin and Garfield, *op. cit.*

[13]Romans 12; 1 Corinthians 12.

[14]Galatians 6:2.

[15]For a discussion of how spiritual and nonspiritual factors play a role in psychopathology, see Collins, Gary R., *Fractured Personalities*. Carol Stream, Illinois: Creation House, 1972.

[16]See, for example, Oates, Wayne E., *When Religion Gets Sick*. Philadelphia: Westminster, 1970.

[17]May, Rollo. *The Art of Counseling*. New York: Abingdon, 1939, p. 218.

[18]Allport, Gordon W. *The Individual and His Religion*. New York: Macmillan, 1950, pp. 90-92.

[19]1 Corinthians 13; 1 John 4:18.

[20]1 John 4:9-11 (The Living Bible).

[21]John 3:16 (The Living Bible).

[22]Matthew 5, 6, 7.

[23]Krishna, Puroshotman M., "Presenting One Way to the Universalist," *Christianity Today* **16,** July 28, 1972, pp. 4-6.

Epilogue

During the time I was in graduate school, a fellow student once made a comment about my religious beliefs. "I just can't figure you out," he said in a good-natured but amazed tone of voice. "Here you are almost finished with your training. You are getting good grades and seem to be 'making it' through the program, but you go to church and still have faith in God. It's unbelievable!"

I understand the amazement of my friend. Psychologists aren't exactly well known for religious fervor, and to find someone in the field who claims to be a convinced Christian is relatively rare. Some psychologists are hostile toward religion and many more are neutral, apparently having concluded that while theology doesn't do any harm, it certainly doesn't contribute anything positive to our understanding of behavior.

In writing this book I have had two groups of people in mind. First and primarily there are those psychologists and students who have a Christian commitment but who are frequently reminded by their colleagues and professors that religion and psychology don't mix. I am convinced that they *do* mix, and that the Christian who pushes his faith aside in deference to psychology is cutting himself off from the only system that can really give meaning and new direction to our discipline. The Christian in psychology is in a unique position to study how psychological science and the Christian faith can be integrated, and to demonstrate by his writing, research, and clinical practice that biblically-based presuppositions

200   make far better sense than the naturalistic and
nonbiblical assumptions that have led psychology to its
present state of widespread irrelevance and
fragmentation. Christians must not abandon the field of
psychology, dismiss it as being of no value, or leave it to
the efforts of non-Christian scholars. Rather, we are
convinced that Jesus Christ and the written Word of God
can exert a powerful positive influence not only on
psychology but on the personal lives of individual
psychologists and on the behavior of those many people
who look to psychology for help and direction. The
Christian psychologist does not believe that he has some
kind of privileged position which lets him understand
and change human behavior better than the nonbeliever.
But the Christian does have a source of truth (the Bible)
that other psychologists tend to overlook, and an
interpreter (the Holy Spirit) who enables us to
understand the truth. It is important that there be
Christians in all professional fields, including
psychology, competent in their scientific skills and
knowledge, convinced of their beliefs, committed to
Christ, consistent in Christian living, and courageous
enough to take a stand for what they believe to be true. It
is also of crucial importance that these same Christians
involve themselves in the work of demonstrating with
every technique available that psychology, built on this
new foundation, is indeed less fragmented than existing
psychology, productive of better research conclusions, and
more effective in its counseling techniques. The burden
of proof is on the one who dares to propose something
new.

   This book is written, therefore, as a stimulus for action
rather than as a report of past progress. Thousands of
psychologists have tried to build their science on the old
foundation, but almost nobody has begun building on
the new. Herein lies an exciting challenge for psychologists
and psychology students in the future. We must keep
consciously aware of the new presuppositions as we plan
our research or counsel with our counselees, and we

201   must work toward building a new psychology that may turn
out to be very different from the old.

A second group I have had in mind during the writing
of this book are those psychologists and psychology
students who are nonbelievers and perhaps have no
personal interest in Christianity. They are sometimes
written off by believers as "atheistic psychologists" who
would never listen to the Christian message even if they
did hear it. I don't believe most of my psychological
colleagues are that narrow-minded. So I have tried to
present biblically-based Christianity in an understandable
fashion and to show that it is a viable alternative to the
often unexamined non-Christian world view that forms the
religion of so many psychologists. Frequently we see
that our colleagues, patients, fellow students, and perhaps
even we ourselves are dissatisfied with life but are
unable to find satisfying answers within psychology.
Around us there is almost a stampede to occultism,
Eastern mysticism, Western ecstasy groups, psychedelic
escapism, cults of Satan worship, and a host of other
movements that claim to offer some meaning to life. In
spite of these proclaimed panaceas, however, many
people today remain frustrated, cynical, despairing, and
vainly searching for some purpose for living. I have
argued that the Christian message is a feasible answer to
the problems of modern men and women. How tragic it
is that antireligious biases and unwillingness to
investigate the facts of Christianity keep so many from
finding the only real source of inner peace, which comes
from commitment of one's life to Jesus Christ.

Most of us who are seriously interested in psychology,
be we amateurs or professionals, find that ours is an
exciting field of study. But it could be better if built on the
basic premise that God exists and is the source of all
truth. I have written this book with the hope that
increasing numbers of psychologists and students will be
willing to build our discipline on this foundation. Even
more, I hope that the readers of these pages, whether or
not they are believers, will be willing to build their

202 personal lives around the person of Jesus Christ, whose character and teachings are revealed in the Bible. He can transform individual psychologists and reshape the future of modern psychology.

Bibliography

The following books, most of which have been mentioned in the text, provide source material for the issues discussed in this book. An asterisk (*) indicates books that the author especially recommends for further study.

Alexander, Dennis. *Beyond Science.* Philadelphia: Holman, 1972.

*Allport, Gordon W. *The Individual and His Religion: A Psychological Interpretation.* New York: Macmillan, 1950.

Anderson, J. N. D. *The Evidence for the Resurrection.* London: Inter-Varsity, 1950.

Beit-Hallahmi, Benjamin. *Research in Religious Behavior: Selected Readings.* Monterey, California: Brooks/Cole, 1973.

Bergin, Allen E. and Garfield, Sol L. (ed.). *Handbook of Psychotherapy and Behavior Change.* New York: Wiley, 1971.

Berkouwer, G. C. *Man: The Image of God.* Grand Rapids: Eerdmans, 1962.

Bloesch, Donald. *The Ground of Certainty.* Grand Rapids: Eerdmans, 1971.

Boring, Edwin G. *A History of Experimental Psychology.* (2nd ed.) New York: Appleton-Century-Crofts, 1950.

*Braginsky, B. M. and Braginsky, D. D. *Mainstream Psychology.* New York: Holt, Rinehart and Winston, 1974.

Brenner, Charles. *An Elementary Textbook of Psychoanalysis.* Garden City, New York: Doubleday, 1957.

Brown, L. B. (ed.) *Psychology and Religion: Selected Readings.* Baltimore: Penguin, 1973.

Bruce, F. F. *The New Testament Documents: Are They Reliable?* Grand Rapids: Eerdmans, 1943.

*Bube, Richard H. *The Human Quest: A New Look at Science and Christian Faith.* Waco, Texas: Word, 1971.

Bube, Richard H. (ed.). *The Encounter Between Christianity and Science.* Grand Rapids: Eerdmans, 1968.

Bugental, J. F. T. (ed.). *Challenges of Humanistic Psychology.* New York: McGraw-Hill, 1967.

Buhler, Charlotte. *Values in Psychotherapy.* New York: Free Press, 1962.

Buhler, Charlotte and Allen, Melanie. *Introduction to Humanistic Psychology.* Monterey, California: Brooks/Cole, 1972.

204

*Carnell, Edward J. *An Introduction to Christian Apologetics.* Grand Rapids: Eerdmans, 1948.

Chein, Isidor. *The Science of Behavior and the Image of Man.* New York: Basic Books, 1972.

Clark, Gordon H., et al. *Can I Trust My Bible?* Chicago: Moody, 1963.

Clark, Gordon H. *Religion, Reason and Revelation.* Nutley, New Jersey: The Craig Press, 1961.

Collins, Gary R. *How to Be a People-Helper.* Santa Ana, California: Vision House, 1976.

*Collins, Gary R. *Search for Reality: Psychology and the Christian.* Santa Ana, California: Vision House, 1969.

Corsini, R. (ed.). *Current Psychotherapies.* Itasca, Illinois: Peacock, 1973.

Coulson, William R. and Rogers, Carl (ed.). *Man and the Science of Man.* Columbus, Ohio: Charles E. Merrill, 1968.

Erikson, Erik H. *Young Man Luther: A Study of Psychoanalysis and History.* New York: Norton, 1958.

Eysenck, H. J. (ed.). *Handbook of Abnormal Psychology.* New York: Basic Books, 1961.

Eysenck, H. J. *The Effects of Psychotherapy.* New York: International Science Press, 1966.

Frankl, V. *Man's Search for Meaning: An Introduction to Logotherapy.* New York: Washington Square Press, 1965.

Freud, Sigmund. *Moses and Monotheism.* London: Hogarth Press, 1964 (1939).

Freud, Sigmund. *Totem and Taboo.* London: Routledge and Kegan Paul, 1950 (1913).

Freud, Sigmund. *The Future of an Illusion.* Garden City, N. Y.: Doubleday, 1927.

Fromm, Erich. *Psychoanalysis and Religion.* New York: Bantam Books, 1950.

Fromm, Erich. *Ye Shall Be as Gods: A Radical Interpretation of the Old Testament and Its Tradition.* New York: Holt, Rinehart and Winston, 1966.

Gaebelein, Frank. *The Pattern of God's Truth.* Chicago: Moody Press, 1968.

Giorgi, Amedeo, *Psychology as a Human Science.* New York: Harper & Row, 1970.

Glasser, William. *Reality Therapy.* New York: Harper & Row, 1965.

Goble, Frank. *The Third Force: The Psychology of Abraham Maslow.* New York: Grossman, 1970.

Grinker, R. R., Sr. *Psychiatry in Broad Perspective.* New York: Behavioral, 1975.

Hall, C. S. and Lindzey, G. *Theories of Personality.* (2nd ed.). New York: Wiley, 1970.

BIBLIOGRAPHY

205

*Hammes, John A. *Humanistic Psychology: A Christian Interpretation*. Grune & Stratton, 1971.

Holmes, Arthur F. *Faith Seeks Understanding*. Grand Rapids: Eerdmans, 1971.

Hudson, Liam. *The Cult of the Fact*. London: Jonathan Cape, 1972.

James, William. *The Varieties of Religious Experience*. Garden City, N. Y.: Dolphin Books, 1902.

*Jeeves, Malcolm A. *The Scientific Enterprise and Christian Faith*. Downers Grove, Illinois: Inter-Varsity Press, 1969.

Keller, Fred S. *The Definition of Psychology: An Introduction to Psychological Systems*. New York: Appleton-Century-Crofts, 1937.

Keller, Werner. *The Bible as History*. New York: William Morrow, 1956.

*MacKay, Donald M. *The Clockwork Image*. Downers Grove, Illinois: Inter-Varsity, 1974.

Maier, Paul L. *First Easter*. New York: Harper & Row, 1973.

Maslow, A. H. *The Farther Reaches of Human Nature*. New York: Viking, 1971.

Matson, Floyd W. *The Broken Image*. New York: Braziller, 1964.

Matson, Floyd W. (ed.). *Without/Within: Behaviorism and Humanism*. Monterey, California: Brooks/Cole, 1973.

*Meehl, P., et al. *What, Then, Is Man?* St. Louis: Concordia, 1958.

Montgomery, John Warwick (ed.). *Christianity for the Tough-Minded*. Minneapolis: Bethany Fellowship, 1973.

Niebuhr, H. Richard. *Christ and Culture*. New York: Harper and Row Publishers, (Harper Torch Books, The Cloister Library), 1951.

Oates, Wayne E. *When Religion Gets Sick*. Philadelphia: Westminster, 1970.

Pattison, E. Mansell (ed.). *Clinical Psychiatry and Religion*. Boston: Little, Brown and Company, 1969.

Paul, G. L. *Insight vs. Desensitization in Psychotherapy*. Stanford: Stanford University Press, 1966.

Pinnock, Clark H. *Biblical Revelation: The Foundation of Christian Theology*. Chicago: Moody, 1971.

*Pinnock, Clark H. *Set Forth Your Case: An Examination of Christianity's Credentials*. Chicago: Moody, 1967.

Progoff, Ira. *The Death and Rebirth of Psychology*. New York: McGraw-Hill, 1956.

Ramm, Bernard. *Protestant Christian Evidences*. Chicago: Moody, 1953.

Ramm, Bernard. *Varieties of Christian Apologetics*. Chicago: Moody, 1961.

Rogers, Carl R. *Carl Rogers on Encounter Groups*. New York: Harper & Row, 1970.

Rosenthal, R. *Experimenter Effects in Behavioral Research*. New York: Appleton, 1966.

206

Rychlak, Joseph F. *A Philosophy of Science for Personality Theory.* Boston: Houghton-Mifflin, 1968.

Schaeffer, Francis A. *Back to Freedom and Dignity.* Downers Grove, Illinois: Inter-Varsity, 1972.

Schaeffer, Francis A. *The God Who Is There.* Chicago: Inter-Varsity, 1968.

*Schultz, Duane P. *The Science of Psychology: Critical Reflections.* New York: Appleton-Century-Crofts, 1970.

Schweitzer, Albert. *The Psychiatric Study of Jesus.* Boston: The Beacon Press, 1948.

Severin, Frank T. (ed.). *Humanistic Viewpoints in Psychology.* New York: McGraw-Hill, 1965.

Severin, Frank T. (ed.). *Discovering Man in Psychology.* New York: McGraw-Hill, 1973.

Skinner, B. F. *Science and Human Behavior.* New York: The Free Press, 1953.

Skinner, B. F. *Beyond Freedom and Dignity.* New York: Alfred A. Knopf, 1971.

Stott, John R. W. *Your Mind Matters: The Place of the Mind in the Christian Life.* Downers Grove, Illinois: Inter-Varsity, 1973.

Tenney, Merrill C. (ed.). *The Bible: The Living Word of Revelation.* Grand Rapids: Zondervan, 1968.

Tenney, Merrill C. *The Reality of the Resurrection.* New York: Harper & Row, 1963.

Thouless, Robert E. *An Introduction to the Psychology of Religion.* (3rd ed.). Cambridge: Cambridge University Press, 1971.

Thomson, Robert. *The Pelican History of Psychology.* Baltimore: Penguin, 1968.

Torrey, E. Fuller. *The Death of Psychiatry.* New York: Penguin, 1974.

Tournier, Paul. *The Person Reborn.* New York: Harper & Row, 1966.

Tweedie, Donald F. *Logotherapy and the Christian Faith: An Evaluation of Frankl's Existential Approach to Psychotherapy.* Grand Rapids: Baker Book House, 1961.

Tweedie, Donald F. *The Christian and the Couch: An Introduction to Christian Logotherapy.* Grand Rapids: Baker Book House, 1963.

Walker, Edward. *Psychology as a Natural and Social Science.* Belmont, California: Brooks/Cole, 1970.

Wann, T. W. (ed.). *Behaviorism and Phenomenology.* Chicago: University of Chicago Press, 1964.

Welford, A. T. *Christianity: A Psychologist's Translation.* London: Hodder and Stoughton, 1971.

*Wertheimer, Michael. *Fundamental Issues in Psychology.* New York: Holt, Rinehart and Winston, 1972.

Wilson, Colin. *New Pathways in Psychology: Maslow and the Post Freudian Revolution.* London: Victor Gollancz, 1972.

Index